Alexander Walsh has practised at national and regional law firms for almost 10 years, specialising in litigation and dispute resolution. He has acted for SME's, major insurers, FTSE 100 retailers and individuals, in wide range of civil and commercial disputes. Alexander was recognised in the 2018 Legal 500 where he was described as having "a great deal of knowledge". He is now in-house Dispute Resolution Counsel for a major food group.

A Practical Guide to Neighbour Disputes and the Law

A Practical Guide to Neighbour Disputes and the Law

Alexander Walsh LL.B (Hons), PG Dip
Solicitor of the Senior Courts of England and Wales

Law Brief Publishing

Published 2020 by Law Brief Publishing, an imprint of Law Brief Publishing Ltd
30 The Parks
Minehead
Somerset
TA24 8BT

www.lawbriefpublishing.com

Paperback: 978-1-912687-53-4

PREFACE

Generally most people want to get along with their neighbours. However, in some situations disagreements between the parties or annoyance can quickly escalate into a dispute. When this happens if the parties are unable to resolve the dispute between themselves they very often turn to lawyers for assistance. As soon as lawyers become involved, the dispute can be tricky to resolve as the longer it runs on, and the more costs are incurred, the likelihood each party will want to settle decreases. Undoubtedly, some people do just want 'their day in court' but when they do often find that they meet with an unsympathetic judge, a large costs bill and an unsalable property. And, whatever the outcome of a case, the losing party will also continue to live next door.

There is commonality with the contemporary and historical authorities in this area; which is that almost all of the disputes should have never gone to court. These disputes must be carefully handled by lawyers and a real effort made to try and settle it as quickly as possible and I hope that this book will be useful to any practitioners dealing with neighbour disputes.

In addition to thanking the team at Law Brief Publishing Ltd, I would also like to thank Ms Stephanie Tozer QC and her co-authors at Falcon Chambers and Hogan Lovells for kindly permitting me to reproduce a copy of the Boundary Disputes Protocol.

Alexander Walsh
January 2020

CONTENTS

INTRODUCTION

The second great commandment provided by Jesus in the Bible is "thou shalt love thy neighbour as thyself"[1]. Whilst this is of course a metaphorical reference to the way in which people should treat each other, its literal sense is also highly appropriate. Unfortunately, despite peoples' best efforts to live in peace, disputes between neighbours can arise and when they do they can prove to be extremely difficult cases to resolve. This book is intended to provide a brief overview as to what common types of disputes can arise and how to deal with them.

Why do such disputes arise? It is beyond the scope of this book to examine the precise causes of neighbour disputes but one possible answer is that they are the by-product of a modern world which is focused on the individual and which is rapidly eroding, if not destroyed completely, the sense of community spirit in the areas where we live.

A survey carried out in 2011 suggested that only 6% of respondents said that there was a strong sense of community where they lived. Shockingly, 70% admitted to not even knowing their neighbours' names. Against that backdrop it is easy to see how a breakdown in communication can take place which is so often the cause of disputes.

The situation has possibly been exacerbated by the housing crisis and with property being so expensive to buy many people are in a 'rent trap'. How can a community maintain, or renew, its spirit if its members are moving in and out of areas every six months or so to the next rental property, never being able to put down roots and get to know their neighbours?

---

1   Matthew 22:36-40 King James Version

Neighbour disputes can arise in a multitude of ways, including disputes over the boundary, obstruction of a right of way, noisy neighbours and damage caused by trees, amongst many others. They can be very difficult to deal with since often the parties become quickly entrenched, fuelled by a combination of emotional energy and close proximity to the dispute. As such, in these circumstances litigants can quickly incur a substantial sum of legal costs which also adds a further layer of difficulty with settlement.

These types of disputes are also renowned for attracting negative judicial treatment, often to the surprise of clients. Whilst this may be just because of the often insignificant subject of the litigation itself, I think that the courts have a deep seated frustration with people wanting to litigate the disputes in the first place, or in other words, a frustration with the litigants themselves and their (or their lawyers') inability to reach a mutually acceptable resolution.

Probably the most famous, and oft quoted, comment concerning this judicial attitude to neighbour disputes is the obiter from Lord Hoffman in the well-known case of *Wibberley v. Insley* [1999] HL15, which concerned a boundary dispute in rural Staffordshire:

> "*Boundary disputes are a particularly painful form of litigation. Feelings run high and disproportionate amounts of money are spent. Claims to small and valueless pieces of land are pressed with the zeal of Fortinbras' army*"[2]

Whatever the judicial attitude to such cases is (and will undoubtedly continue to harden) it is clear that these types of disputes are not going to go away. And with the need to build more houses and housing estates to help address the housing crisis it is possible that they could even increase.

---

2   Wibberley v. Insley [1999] HL15

There is light at the end of the tunnel, however, in the form of future reform. The Property Boundaries (Resolution of Disputes) Bill which had its first reading in the House of Lords on 13th July 2017 would implement a new system of resolving such disputes by way of expert determination but has since been stalled by the pro-roguing of Parliament connected with Brexit.

There is also a voluntary protocol by which to deal with boundary disputes, called the Protocol for Disputes between Neighbours about the Location of their Boundary drafted by members of Falcon Chambers and Hogan Lovells which has designed a process by which parties to a boundary dispute can resolve it by the provision of notice and disclosure of documents followed by the joint instruction of a surveyor with the aim of resolution being achieved without needing to commence court proceedings.

It is unclear when there will be further progress with the bill but it is without doubt a welcome, and positive, development in an attempt to change the present unsatisfactory system of resolution by litigation and the often ruinous costs implications that come with it.

As I have stated above this book intends to briefly examine the most common types of disputes and provide a practical guide as to how such cases can be addressed and resolved. It is, however, not intended to be exhaustive and practitioners are also recommended to consult more specialist texts, such as *Megarry and Wade: The Law of Real Property* and *Gale on Easements*.

I have endeavoured to state the law as at 20th December 2019.

CHAPTER ONE
BOUNDARY DISPUTES

1. <u>Introduction</u>

One of the most common ways a dispute can arise between neighbours is where there is a dispute concerning the boundary between their respective titles (whether this be a property itself or the land). Unfortunately, in many cases the land in question can be insignificant and the dispute compounded by the parties misunderstanding of what is shown in Land Registry title plans. Disputes like this should be approached with caution and handled with care as there is often no satisfactory conclusion for either party.

If you have not been a litigant in a boundary dispute before it is perhaps hard to see the psychology behind why such disputes occur. One possible answer could be that peoples' properties are their homes and any event or intrusion which affects the status quo or intrinsic feeling of security of that "home" is a much more personal affront than it may be to an outsider. This is made even worse when the perpetrator of the event or intrusion is your own neighbour. What is clear, however, is that once a boundary dispute arises it is very difficult to resolve. Many clients will say that they will simply move house to avoid the stress and hassle of dealing with the dispute but subsequently find that they cannot do so without declaring the existence of the dispute, or the moving of a boundary, to any potential buyers in the Sellers Property Information Form.

It is unlikely that in the majority of cases the actions of the 'aggressor' neighbour are with the intention of unlawfully stealing land which does not belong to them but even if that was the case they are unlikely to admit it.

More often than not their actions can be explained, and put down to, a lack of understanding as to what is shown by their title plan and a belief that it shows precisely where the boundary is located. That belief, however, is a fallacy.

2. The General Boundaries rule

England and Wales differ from many countries by operating what is called a 'general boundaries' system of land registration. Section 60 (1) of the Land Registration Act 2002 is where the modern source of the 'general boundaries rule' is located.

When it was enacted the Land Registration Act 2002 preserved the existing position provided for by Rule 278 of the Land Registration Rules 1925[1] which stated:

> "*Except in cases in which it is noted in the Property Register that the boundaries have been fixed, the filed plan shall be deemed to indicate the general boundaries only*"[2].

The effect of section 60, and the meaning of the rule, is that unless the boundaries have been defined, Land Registry title plans will only be *indicative* and therefore not an absolutely precise measurement or plan. There will be a degree of slippage. A title plan only shows a general boundary and a general boundary does not establish the legal boundary.

Therefore, a title plan cannot (and, importantly, is not intended to) be an accurate representation of where a boundary is located on the ground. Despite this the title plan and any deeds (specifically looking at the description of the conveyed land and any plans) is the most

---

1   Which in turn preserved the earlier provisions in the Land Transfer Act 1875

2   Rule 278 (1)

logical starting point in a boundary dispute since if they are unclear it will help give some indication as to the general location and extent of the boundary and be the basis upon which further enquiries can be made.

3. Boundary Features

If the plan is from Ordnance Survey then for boundary features the general rule is that the boundary line will run through the middle of that feature. However, as part of the investigative process it is vitally important to actually visit the site in question (or at the very least see good photographs) to see the lay of the land and to also note any physical features which may provide an insight into the location of the boundary and whether or not it could have moved[3]. This is particularly important in circumstances where either the plan or transfer is unclear[4].

Common boundary features include trees, hedges, fences and walls.

Trees and hedges

Any trees and hedges located on a boundary will be deemed to be owned by the person who planted it[5]. If, however, the hedge is very old and the identity of whoever planted it is unclear, it has been suggested that any action taken in relation to the maintenance of the hedge can be used as evidence to indicate possible ownership[6]. It is

---

3 Which may give rise to adverse possession or estoppel arguments

4 In Cameron v. Boggiano and another [2012] EWCA Civ 157 the court permitted consideration of physical features present on the date the land was transferred when considering the extent of a title plan.

5 Lemmon v. Webb [1894] 3 Ch 1

6 Davey v. Harrow Corporation [1958] 1 QB 60

also possible for trees to become jointly owned if the roots and branches grow onto the adjoining land[7].

Walls

If a wall has been built along a boundary then it will be jointly owned, with each owner owning the 'half' of the wall which is on their land. In this situation then the wall will also be a party wall which has implications in the event that one of the owners wishes to carry out works on, or near to, the wall as a prescribed procedure must be followed before the works can commence (see Chapter 3).

If a wall is not built directly on the boundary then it will be owned by the party on whose land it has been built, but rights concerning it could be acquired by an adjoining owner either by agreement or pre-scription, such as a right to support if the wall had been used as part of the adjoining owners building.

Fences

If a dispute concerns a fence then it will be necessary to see the land and fence in question and to establish the historical background. A fence will be owned by the person who erected it, but some fences may have the posts on one side and the boards on the other, or a different construction to other fences on the same land or to fences on adjoining land, which is not helpful in providing an insight as to the identity of the person who put the fence up if it is unknown. In such a situation, it had been considered that the ownership could be established simply by looking at the fence because the side with the posts would face the owners land and the side with the boarding would face towards the neighbour's land. However, there is no legal foundation to this and it can clearly be envisaged that most people

---

7 Waterman v. Soper [1698] 1 Ld Raym 737

will not want the side with the boarding facing their neighbours land as that it would remove the aesthetic aspect.

It is also important to be aware of any 'T' marks on plans or maps as these may indicate ownership of a boundary feature including fences, with the top of the 'T' pointing towards the owner[8]. However, a site visit may reveal that there is no longer any feature, or it has been replaced (and even moved) by the owner or another. Therefore, whilst such indications can be useful it does not negate the need for a site visit.

4. Rebuttable Presumptions

If the boundary is not clear from the title deeds then there are also a number of rebuttable presumptions which can assist in locating the boundary.

Highways

Where land adjoins a highway then there is a presumption that the owner of that land will own the sub-soil up to the middle of the road. This presumption is known as the *usque ad medium filium viae* presumption.

Rivers and Streams

If land is adjacent to a non-tidal river[9] or stream then the same presumption will apply with the implication that the owner of that land will also own the bed and bank of the river/stream up to the middle point. If the position of the river/stream changes naturally over time then the presumption will follow the change. There is, however, no

---

8 T marks can also indicate a repairing liability

9 Tidal rivers form part of the Crown Estate

application of this presumption applying to a lake which is not entirely within the land of one party.

The 'Hedge and Ditch Rule'

The 'hedge and ditch' rule is a rebuttable presumption mainly applying to fields which provides that if the boundary between two parcels of land consists of a bank and a ditch, it is presumed the legal boundary between the two is the land on the other side of the ditch, opposite the bank. This is the position even if the title plan shows the general boundary line ending on the side with the bank on it, which it is likely to if there is a hedge on the top of the bank, since the Land Registry will use the centreline of that hedge to indicate the boundary.

The basis of the hedge and ditch rule is found in *Vowles v. Miller* where it was stated:

> "*The rule about ditching is this. No man, making a ditch, can cut into his neighbour's soil, but usually he cuts it to the very extremity of his own land*[10]: *he is of course bound to throw the soil which he digs out, upon his own land; and often, if he likes it, he plants a hedge on the top of it*"[11]

However, it is important to be aware that for this presumption to apply there must be, or have been, a bank thereby indicating how the ditch came into existence.

Historically, it also used to be required that the ditch in question must have been created as a feature to mark the boundary but since

---

10 It is presumed that the ditch is dug once the boundary has been ascertained

11 Vowles v. Miller [1810] 3 Taunt 137

the decision in the case of *Parmar & Others v Upton*[12] that is no longer the case.

Parmar concerned a claim for trespass to a boundary, as Mr Parmar had, as part of development works, partially filled in a ditch which ran along the boundary line and into garden land of a new housing development. In considering the evidence the court also found that a hedge had ran alongside the ditch on Mr Upton's side. By applying the hedge and ditch rule and considering a plan from a 1925 conveyance the court subsequently found in Mr Upton's favour. However, after the trial Mr Parmar adduced historic evidence that the ditch had run across land which had been in common ownership until 1920 and appealed the decision on the basis that (a) the presumption had in fact been rebutted as it had not been dug to mark a boundary and (b) by reference to a plan that Mr Upton's title went to the hedge but no further meaning that the ditch belonged to Mr Parmar.

The appeal was, however, dismissed. Lord Justice Briggs stated:

> *"Nothing in the authorities about the hedge and ditch rule show that it is a necessary part of the underlying presumptions that the ditch was dug as a boundary ditch, ie to demarcate a boundary, rather than as a drainage ditch"*[13]

He also went on to say:

> *"On the contrary, farmers generally dig and then maintain ditches at not inconsiderable expense for the economic purpose of draining farmland so as to improve its yield, whether as arable or pasture, rather than for the anxious purpose of the precise defining of their boundaries with their neighbours. Nothing in the classic*

---

12 Parmar & Others v Upton [2015] EWCA Civ 795

13 At 32

> *description of the second presumption by Laurence J in Vowles v Miller (1810) 3 Taunt 137, at 138, suggests otherwise. The farmer is digging the ditch at the extremity of his own land because he must not cut into his neighbour's soil. Indeed, the first presumption suggests that the farmer already knows where the boundary is, and has no need to mark it out."[14]*

The Court of Appeal found that the ditch in question had been dug by Mr Upton's predecessor at the extremity of their land and therefore the evidence submitted was insufficient to rebut the presumption. The second ground of appeal based on the plan was also dismissed as the plan in question had been marked for identification purposes only and therefore was not for the purpose of identifying the boundary.

The decision in *Parmar* is important as it is no longer required to establish when relying on the presumption that the ditch was created to mark the boundary, or, seemingly, that there even needs to be an existing hedge.

5. <u>Boundary Agreements</u>

In some cases the parties may have already, or previously, reached an agreement as to where the boundary is. An agreement of this nature can of course be at one end of the scale a simple verbal or 'gentlemen's agreement' all the way to a formal documented boundary agreement together with an accurate supporting plan prepared by a surveyor.

Regrettably, however, even where there has been an agreement there is a potential for disputes to arise. For example, one of the parties to the agreement could decide that they no longer wish to comply with

---

14 Ibid

the terms, or a subsequent purchaser may decide to not comply as they do not consider themselves to be bound by terms agreed with a previous owner and/or believes that the agreement is invalid.

The leading case remains *Neilson v. Poole*[15], which concerned an oral agreement which defined the boundary. In that case, it was identified that boundary agreements could take two forms; firstly, those which involve an exchange of land and secondly, those which simply intended to identify the boundary from the general boundary. The court found that, unless there was evidence to the contrary, if parties agree a boundary then this will be an agreement as to the location of a boundary, rather than an agreement to convey land.

This was developed further by the case of *Joyce v. Rigolli*[16] where the Court of Appeal found that a boundary agreement intended to identify and record a boundary should not be treated as a contract to transfer land even if that agreement involved the actual exchange of land so long as the land being exchanged was de minimis.

That decision was in turn reinforced by the High Court in 2012 in the case of *Yeates & Anor v Line & Anor*[17] where the Judge, Mr Kevin Prosser QC, stated:

> "*I conclude that the compromise agreement is not an agreement "for the sale or other disposition of an interest in land" within the meaning of section 2(1) of the 1989 Act, so that despite being oral it is a valid contract*"[18].

The position is now clear that any boundary agreement whether oral or in writing which has been entered into for the purpose of identi-

15 Neilson v. Poole (1969) 20 P. & C.R. 909 (26 February 1969)

16 Joyce v. Rigolli [2004] EWCA Civ 79

17 Yeates & Anor v Line & Anor [2012] EWHC 3085 (Ch) (12 November 2012)

18 At [37]

fying and agreeing a boundary will be valid and will not have to comply with the requirements of section 2 of the Law of Property (Miscellaneous Provisions) Act 1989, even if it involves small pieces of land being exchanged.

Furthermore, any such agreement which has been entered into will bind a subsequent purchaser regardless of whether or not the agreement has been protected by way of registration as an agreed, or unilateral notice, with HM Land Registry. This will also be the position even if the agreement expressly states that it isn't intended to be.

A purchaser of land seeking to challenge a pre-existing boundary agreement should be advised of the inherent difficulty and unattractiveness in challenging such an agreement. In *Haycocks v. Neville*[19] a purchaser of a property which had been the subject of a boundary agreement sought to dispute the terms of that agreement and the location of the boundary. The claim, however, was dismissed on appeal with the court finding that the previous plan which had been agreed by the parties *"should not be ignored and gave an indication of where the boundary was to be found on the developed site"*[20] before going on to say (as can be said for most boundary disputes) *"any solution in this case would be imperfect and that it was a case which should never have come to court"*[21].

6. Applications for a Determined Boundary

An alternative to entering into a boundary agreement is for the parties to apply to HM Land Registry for the boundary to be determined pursuant to section 60 of the Land Registration Act

---

19 Haycocks & Anor v Neville & Anor [2007] EWCA Civ 78

20 At [31]

21 At [32]

2002. This process can be distinguished from the former as a boundary agreement, whilst potentially can be quick and low cost, will only record the agreement. If the Land Registry determines the boundary then this determination will be recorded on the title plan itself with accurate measurements. This method may also have the advantage of minimising applications for adverse possession, as may not be the case with a boundary agreement.

Historically, this process was rarely used because the applicant had to pay the costs of the Land Registry surveyor for surveying the land, which were expensive. However, the new process is more user friendly. Applicants are required to complete Form DB and submit this to the Land Registry together with an accurate plan identifying the boundary on a scale of no less than 1/200, with measurements being accurate to 10mm[22]. If the Land Registry is satisfied with the application and plan it will then give the adjoining owners notice and they in turn will have a period of 20 business days[23] from the date of issue by which to submit their comments.

As is the usual position with applications to the Land Registry if no objection is received the application will be granted and an entry made on all affected titles. If a dispute arises then it will be referred on to the Land Registration Division of the Property Chamber, First-tier Tribunal[24] for resolution. These proceedings will be stayed, however, if one of the parties subsequently commences proceedings in the civil courts pending the outcome of those proceedings.

---

22 See Sections 118-123 of The Land Registration Rules 2003

23 Section 119 (3) of The Land Registration Rules 2003

24 The First-tier Tribunal replaced the role of Adjudicator to the Land Registry on 1st July 2013

7. <u>Remedies</u>

It is widely acknowledged that boundary disputes can be emotionally charged, bitter, disputes which can be difficult to successfully resolve. Any prospective litigant in such a dispute is likely to be faced with a significant level of costs, general litigation and costs risk and an often unsympathetic judiciary.

Furthermore, in some cases the client may say that the matter is (or it may become during the lifecycle of the case), one 'of principle', which further complicates prospects of a successful resolution as well as often resulting in the costs becoming completely disproportionate to the extent of the land involved.

There are several remedies available in a boundary dispute.

Self-help / Abatement

If a neighbour has erected a fence or some other object on the boundary which has caused a nuisance and/or encroachment then it is open to the innocent party to physically remove the object from the land to their neighbour's to abate the nuisance. In doing so, the party must be careful and use reasonable care to do no more damage than is necessary.

However, exercising a self-help remedy in such a dispute is high-risk and not advisable in all but the most clear-cut of cases. This is because by taking action to abate the nuisance the innocent party runs a risk of being sued for trespass and if insufficient care is taken even potentially being liable for criminal damage. It is also worth bearing in mind that the practical effect of such actions may also simply inflame tensions even further.

Self-help should therefore only really be considered in extremely simple cases which would not merit the costs of formal legal action[25] and where there is a degree of urgency, which is not something which can be said for most boundary disputes.

Alternative Dispute Resolution ('ADR')

Alternative Dispute Resolution or 'ADR' is a term used to describe the various methods of resolving disputes without recourse to litigation. ADR as a whole has grown in importance and popularity over the years since the Jackson Reforms in 2013 and is now a key part of any case strategy owing to the possibility of costs sanctions being imposed in the event that a party unreasonably refuses to engage in such a process. Therefore, at least some form of it will take place in almost all disputes and parties are strongly encouraged by the Practice Direction on Pre-Action Conduct to explore this prior to issuing proceedings which should be a last resort and the parties should be considering settlement at all times. A more detailed consideration of ADR can be found in Chapter 8.

The Boundary Disputes Protocol

In September 2017 the Property Litigation Association together with lawyers from Falcon Chambers and Hogan Lovells published The Protocol for Disputes between Neighbours about the Location of their Boundary (The Boundary Disputes Protocol). The Boundary Disputes Protocol is, at the time of writing, presently in draft form and only voluntary but has been introduced in an effort to reform the current system of resolving boundary disputes in favour of the joint instruction of a surveyor with the aim of resolving the matter at a very early stage without needing to issue proceedings.. If voluntarily adopted by the parties, the Protocol is likely to reduce the

---

25 Such as the lopping off of an overhanging branch as was suggested in Burton v. Winters [1993] 1 W.L.R 1077

excessive cost and delay associated with the current process, but it is unclear at the moment to what extent costs sanctions would apply if an invitation to voluntarily adopt the Protocol is refused. A copy of the Boundary Disputes Protocol can be found at Appendix A.

Litigation

If informal attempts to resolve the dispute are unsuccessful and an application is not made to the Land Registry for a determined boundary (which if objected to will end up before the First-Tier Tribunal) then proceedings can be issued in the civil courts with the usual remedies sought including, an injunction, an order for possession of the land, a declaration and/or damages.

Of course, litigation should be a last resort and any prospective litigant should be made aware of the inherent dangers of commencing litigation in such circumstances at an early stage, with the Courts even going so far as to say that there is a professional duty on the party's lawyers to advise them as such. In the case of *Wilkinson v. Farmer*[26] LJ Mummery clearly explained the judicial attitude to neighbour litigation (that case concerned a disagreement over the width of a right of way) and paragraph four of the judgment a useful passage to bring to the client's attention, and states:

> "*The whole exercise has been an uncomfortable experience of unsatisfactory aspects of the conduct and cost of neighbour disputes in the courts. Everybody agrees that, if at all possible, disagreements between neighbours about rights of way, boundaries or whatever should be settled without ever going near a court. In my view, professional advisers have a duty to warn their clients at an early stage about the downside of neighbour litigation, even for a successful party. If the case goes to court there is, as this case shows, some uncertainty about the ultimate outcome. The case does not*

---

26 [2010] EWCA Civ 1148

always end with the trial. Appeals are possible. What is certain is that, at the end of the day, one of the parties will lose and will usually finish up fixed with an order to pay very considerable legal costs. That is not good for the losing party or for the prospect of harmonious relations between neighbours who continue to live next door to each other after the case is over. The cost and stress of a court case will often result in the further deterioration of already damaged relationships. The parties might be horrified to discover that the litigation has blighted their properties, as well as their lives".

The landscape of litigation has undergone a major change in the years following the Jackson Reforms in April 2013. Cases are now actively managed by the court and the implementation of costs budgeting has enabled litigants to see in advance what the potential costs liability could be at a relatively early stage in the process. The authors own experience of costs budgeting is that the process can result in two outcomes; either it gives the parties a 'reality check' as to how much it will cost if they end up losing the case and provides a spring board to settlement discussions, or, conversely, can even have the effect of encouraging a party to proceed with the litigation as they know, and are comfortable with, the amount of costs they will have to pay will be if they lose. The knowledge that absent an unforeseen development (in which case budgets can be revised) the opponent will not be able to claim any more costs than their approved budget if they win, provides a level of certainty which is not always conducive to settlement.

Prior to issuing proceedings, the claimant must send a letter of claim which contains *"concise details of the claim. The letter should include the basis on which the claim is made, a summary of the facts, what the claimant wants from the defendant, and if money, how the amount is calculated"*[27].

---

27 Pre-Action Protocol on Pre-Action Conduct, s.6 (a)

The defendant must then respond, generally, within a period of 14-21 days unless the matter is particularly complex, in which case a response can be sent up to 3 months from receiving the letter. The response must indicate whether or not the claim is accepted, and if not, setting out reasons why. The parties should also disclose any documents with the respective letters, including any expert reports which have been obtained.

Issuance

If the dispute has not settled following the letter of claim and the response then the next step is to issue court proceedings, which is covered by Civil Procedure Rule 7 and Practice Direction 7A.

In the vast majority of cases the appropriate venue for issuance will be the local County Court, which has very wide jurisdiction[28]. The High Court is only an appropriate venue for issuance if there is a money claim is excess of £100,000[29], or:

"if by reason of:

(1) the financial value of the claim and the amount in dispute, and/or

(2) the complexity of the facts, legal issues, remedies or procedures involved, and/or

(3) the importance of the outcome of the claim to the public in general,

---

28 See section 38 of the County Courts Act 1984, as amended by the Courts and Legal Services Act 1990 and the High Court and County Court Jurisdiction Order 1991 (SI 199/724)

29 PD7A 2.1

the claimant believes that the claim ought to be dealt with by a High Court judge"[30]

There is also a requirement that possession claims can only be issued in the High Court if the requirements in PD55A are met. Possession claims should also be issued in the county court which is local to the disputed property, and if they aren't the court should transfer them there[31] (although the court may just return the proceedings unsealed) which will result in delay. In order to ascertain the appropriate venue contact should be made the nearest court to see if the property is within their area, or if not, which court is.

A court fee is also payable to issue proceedings the amount of which can be found in leaflet EX50[32]. For claims seeking possession of land a court fee of £355.00 is payable, for non-money claims the court fee is £308.00 and any claims for damages will attract a fee on a sliding scale depending on value. For damages claims over £200,000, or importantly, if the claim for damages is uncapped, a court fee of £10,000 is payable. In circumstances where a number of remedies are being sought the court will usually require the court fees for each remedy paid together before issuance and if the proceedings have been issued without the appropriate fee(s) being paid then an application can be made for a stay pending those fees being paid[33].

---

30 PD7A 2.4

31 CPR r.55.3 (1) (c)

32 https://assets.publishing.service.gov.uk/government/uploads/system/uploads/attach
ment_data/file/789201/ex50-eng.pdf

33 Lifestyles Equities CV & Anor v Sportsdirect.com Retail Ltd & Ors [2016] EWHC 2092 (Ch)

A Civil Claim: A Brief Overview

Once proceedings have been issued then the defendant will have 14 days to file an acknowledgment of service indicating whether or not they intend to defend all of the claim, part of the claim or dispute the court's jurisdiction. This will also give the defendant an additional 14 days to file a defence. If the defence also includes a counterclaim then a defence to counterclaim should be filed to prevent the defendant from requesting that judgment be entered. The claimant can then file a reply to defence.

Once the statements of case have all been filed, the court will send the parties a directions questionnaire which is completed and returned with draft directions. The purpose of the directions questionnaire is to provide the court with sufficient information by which to allocate the claim to a particular track. In cases where the parties have indicated that they are seeking different tracks, or cannot agree directions, the court will list a case management conference ('CMC') during which they court will hear submissions from the parties and following which the case will then be allocated and directions given.

If the court proposes that the case is allocated to the multi-track then the directions questionnaire and draft directions will also need to be accompanied with a costs budget[34]. Following this the court will then list a costs and case management conference ('CCMC') where in addition to providing directions the court will make a costs order.

The failure to file a costs budget on time carries the serious sanction of being treated as only having filed a budget for court fees[35]. In those circumstances an urgent application for relief from sanctions must be made with the supporting evidence addressing the three-

---

34 See CPR r.3.13 (1) (a) and (b).

35 CPR 3.14

stage test set out in *Denton & Ors v TH White [2014] EWCA Civ 906*.

The first major procedural step following the CMC or CCMC is called disclosure. This is usually commenced with the parties providing each other with a list of documents setting out what documents they hold which are both advantageous and disadvantageous to their case. The parties can then request sight of any of the documents set out in the list, which usually must be provided within 7-14 days from the date of the request, failing which an application for specific disclosure can be made.

Following disclosure the parties will exchange witness statements from any witnesses of fact on which they intend to rely. This is followed by the disclosure of any report(s) from expert witnesses which the parties have been given permission to rely on. In boundary disputes it is common for such evidence to be given by way of a report from a chartered land surveyor who has been instructed on a single joint basis, but in some cases the court will have given permission for both parties to instruct their own expert. Once the report has been disclosed the parties have an opportunity to ask questions for the purposes of clarifying anything in it which may be unclear.

The provision of answers to any questions will conclude the main procedural stages of the claim and the next step will be for the trial of the case to take place. Trials take place in public before a single judge and may last for several days with judgment either being provided on the day but in complex cases may be 'reserved' and handed down following the trial. The judgment will also include an order dealing with costs.

Costs in neighbour disputes

Any litigation is expensive. This is doubly so for the unsuccessful litigant since they will usually be ordered to pay the costs of their successful opponent (either on the standard or indemnity basis) as well as having to pay for their own lawyers.

Although historically a successful party could usually expect to recover between 60-70% of their legal costs from the unsuccessful party, for contemporary cases which are subject to costs budgeting this has now changed. Rule 3.18 (b) states that if a costs management order has been made the Court will "*not depart from such approved or agreed budgeted costs unless satisfied that there is good reason to do so*" and therefore the only scope for reducing an opponent's costs will be to challenge the level of any costs incurred prior to the costs management order (which will relate to pre-action costs, statements of case and costs incurred in relation to preparing for the Costs and Case Management Conference). If a costs budget has been approved then any unsuccessful litigant seeking to challenge their successful opponent's costs upon conclusion of the case will face an uphill struggle to reduce them from the approved figures.

There have been a number of cases relating to neighbour disputes over the past few years which have been the subject of strong criticism by the judiciary on the level of costs being incurred. It is perhaps helpful to explore a small handful of these in further detail as they could be useful examples to cite to clients when they are considering whether or not to commence litigation.

In *Gilks & Anor v. Hodgson & Anor*[36] which was a case heard by the Court of Appeal in 2015 and which concerned whether the Claimants' property had a right of way to a public highway over a lane belonging to the defendants, Lord Justice Bean stated:

---

36 [2015] EWCA Civ 5

"I only add how dismayed I have been by this Dickensian litigation. The disputed strip of land and right of way do not constitute the sole means of access to anyone's home. The award of damages to Mr & Mrs Gilks was £3,500. Yet, at a time when the courts are under great pressure, the battle between these two couples took up ten days of court time – more than some murder trials – before Judge Armitage and a further three days in this court; and about half a million pounds has been spent in costs. It is almost as though Lord Woolf and other civil procedure reformers over the years have laboured in vain."[37]

Whilst not a case concerning a boundary dispute *Court v Van Dijk & Anor*[38] was a claim for nuisance arising from alleged unlawful interference with the usage of a shared common private drain in York, North Yorkshire. The dispute itself centred on who should pay for work which had been carried out to the drain. The case was initially decided in 2013 with York County Court awarding damages of £4,227.88 plus interest to the Defendant. It was subsequently appealed by Mrs Court and was heard by the Court of Appeal on 5th May 2016. Giving judgment, Lord Justice Floyd stated:

"Whilst it has no bearing on the issues which we have had to decide, it is a regrettable feature of this case that the litigation continues only because of the enormous sums in costs which are at stake. It is said that Mrs Court now faces a costs bill from the other parties of some £220,000. Mrs Court has herself expended very large sums on her own costs: we were told that they were some £89,000. We do not know where the blame lies. Nevertheless, the adjective "disproportionate" is wholly inadequate to describe the combined expenditure on resolving the question of who pays a £4,000 bill."[39]

---

37 At [42]

38 [2016] EWCA Civ 483

39 At [1]

Finally, *Bradford & Anor v Keith James & Ors*[40] was a case from 2008 which concerning a dispute over a cobbled area of land just 3.7m wide. Lord Justice Mummery said:

> "*There are too many calamitous neighbour disputes in the courts. Greater use should be made of the services of local mediators, who have specialist legal and surveying skills and are experienced in alternative dispute resolution. An attempt at mediation should be made right at the beginning of the dispute and certainly well before things turn nasty and become expensive. By the time neighbours get to court it is often too late for court-based ADR and mediation schemes to have much impact. Litigation hardens attitudes. Costs become an additional aggravating issue. Almost by its own momentum the case that cried out for compromise moves onwards and upwards to a conclusion that is disastrous for one of the parties, possibly for both.*"[41]

---

40 [2008] EWCA Civ 837

41 At [1]

CHAPTER TWO
RIGHTS OF WAY

1. Introduction

Disputes can also commonly arise in situations where one property has the advantage of a right of way over another and that right is in some way interfered with or prevented from being exercised. Such rights, a species of easement, can take myriad of forms and can be absolute or limited in scope. A typical example could be that Party A has a right of access over a driveway owned by Party B in order to access their property (without which access would not be possible) and that the right allowed access at all times and for all purposes, with or without vehicles. In the event that Party A's access is prevented by Party B blocking the driveway and preventing access then that would amount to interference with that right and is actionable.

There is a distinction between an express right of way granted by deed (which would be an 'easement') and a simple, or 'bare', license.

License

A license is simply defined as permission granted orally or in writing without consideration which allows the licensee access which, without the permission, would amount to trespass. A license is the least onerous way for a landowner to grant another party lawful access since it can be revoked immediately at any point without the requirement to give notice and can therefore be of varying duration.

Easements

An easement is a legal interest in land belonging to another. They can be acquired in several ways including by way of an express grant by deed, implied grant and by prescription. A detailed consideration of the creation and acquisition and extinguishments of easements is, however, beyond the scope of this book and for further information reference should be made to specialist texts such as *Gale on Easements*.

Profits à Prendre

Closely linked to easements are profits à prendre, which are rights to take something else from the others land and can include minerals, timber, fish (which is known as profit of piscary) and to exercise sporting rights, including the right to kill animals such as game. If a party with the benefit of a profit[1] is being prevented from exercising it then that right can also be enforced in the same way as an easement for a right of way which has been interfered with and is unable to be exercised.

2. Interference

For interference with a private right of way to be actionable, the interference with the use of the right of way must be substantial. What is 'substantial' will of course depend on the facts of each case, but, generally and practically, must have the effect of either severely restricting, or completely preventing, the right of way from being used whether at all or temporarily.

In *B&Q plc v. Liverpool and Lancashire Properties Limited*[2] the Court were required to consider what would amount to a substantial interference to an express right of way. In that case, B&Q had applied for an injunction restraining the defendant from constructing a 3,500

---

1 'Profit' is a common shorthand reference to profits a prendre

2 (2001) 81 P & CR 20, [2000] EWHC 463 (Ch), [2001] 1 EGLR 92, [2001] 15 EG 138, [2000] EG 101

square foot extension to the rear of its industrial unit which B&Q claimed would affect its right of way. The court granted the injunction and held that the test was not whether what would be left taking into account the interference would be reasonable, but rather whether it was reasonable to insist on usage of what had been granted. If, after the interference, it would not be possible to exercise the right as substantially and practically as before, (or to use Mr Justice Blackburne's words *"rendered materially less convenient"*[3]) then it is likely that substantial interference has occurred.

There have been several cases on the issue of whether a locked gate may amount to a substantial interference. In *Kingsgate Development Projects Ltd v Jordan and another*[4], the Court found that three gates all within 100m of each other on an access track amounted to a substantial interference and ordered one of them to be removed.

The starting point in any event is to consider the nature of the right of way and wording of any operative conveyance, including any plans, including whether the party complaining of the interference has the benefit of it.

3. Change of Use and Excessive Use

A dispute may also arise not in relation to the right of way being unable to be used but rather that the right is being used excessively or for something which is not permitted under the terms of the grant, such as the use of a right of way for access to a single dwelling for access to transport materials for constructing a new dwelling adjacent to it.

---

3 Ibid

4 [2017] EWHC 343 (TCC)

The starting point in such a position is to consider the wording of the grant or the right of way. It may be that the usage is plainly in breach of the terms, particularly if it was a limited grant. However, if the right is unlimited then any increased usage would only be actionable in nuisance if it is excessive and whether or not it is excessive will depend on the facts. The remedy in such a situation is to apply to court for an injunction restraining the excessive use and the dominant owner will be liable in trespass.

Increased usage can also be stopped if the right of way was obtained by prescription if the burden of the increased usage has been caused by a major change in the dominant land[5]. In those circumstances the party with the benefit of the right should either seek to obtain an express grant for the increased usage or to wait until the additional use has been exercised without force, without secrecy and without permission for a period of at least 20 years so as to be also acquired by prescription.

4. Remedies for Interference

In the event that the interference in question is considered to be able to satisfy the test of being substantial then the there are four remedies available for the innocent party to seek, aside from alternative dispute resolution.

Self-help / abatement

The first is self-help (or abatement) which has been explained in the previous chapter. In this context this would entail physically moving of the cause of the interference to enable the right of way to be used again. For example, the physical removal of a locked gate, or the towing away of a parked vehicle blocking a track. However, caution

---

5 McAdams Homes Ltd v. Robinson [2004] EWCA 214

must be exercised when considering this approach as it could give rise to disputes over whether the party exercising self-help did so in a reasonable manner (or used excess force in doing so) and whether any unnecessary damage was caused as part of the process.

Declaration

The first 'court based' remedy is to apply for a declaration from the court as to the extent of the right of way. The purpose behind seeking declaratory relief is that in some cases settlement can be achieved by the court giving its view on the extent of a right of way which would then result with the unsuccessful party abiding by the outcome and acting accordingly, as well as providing certainty for the future. There is also another benefit to seeking a declaration which is that the declaration will be binding on the parties' successors in title, and not just the parties themselves.

Injunction

An injunction is the only one of the four remedies for interference which will actually require action to be taken by the party causing the interference in the event that it is granted.

However, the granting of an injunction is not a guaranteed outcome since an injunction is an equitable remedy which is granted at the Court's discretion and will not be granted in circumstances where the claimant would be adequately compensated by an award of damages. It can also be defeated if there has been extensive delay in making the application[6]. It is often worth reminding clients that injunctions are the exception rather than the rule owing to their draconian nature and the severe repercussions which can apply if breached, which includes committal for contempt.

---

6 The doctrine and defence of **laches** provides that an equitable remedy (such as an injunction) allowing a claimant to enforce their legal rights should not be granted owing to the claimants delay in applying to do so.

Claim for Damages

The final remedy is a simple claim for damages, which can be brought to compensate for any loss which has been suffered as a result of the interference. Such damages are calculated on the tortious basis and will therefore be subject to the usual rules on remoteness and a duty to mitigate.

CHAPTER THREE
RIGHTS OF ACCESS
& PARTY WALLS

1. Introduction

In some circumstances it is not possible to carry out works of repair or improvement to a property without going onto a neighbouring property in order to do so. However, as is similar to the position with rights of light (see Chapter Four), there is no general right at common law[1] to enter onto a neighbouring property. Therefore, the party who requires access will be unable to go onto their neighbours property without trespassing unless either the neighbour provides their consent to the access or there is an easement in place which allows them to do so, since if an easement has been expressly granted then there will be ancillary rights attached, including a right of access for any maintenance and improvement[2], so that the easement can be used.

2. Access to Neighbouring Land Act 1992

So if there isn't an easement and no consent is forthcoming, what can the party do? In those circumstances it is possible to apply via the Part 8 process for an access order under section 1 of the Access to Neighbouring Land Act 1992 ('ANLA'), which if granted will require the uncooperative party to allow the other party access to their land.

---

1 There may be a statutory right of access, for example, under the Party Wall etc. Act 1996

2 A right of way acquired by prescription would differ from a right of way granted expressly for all purposes as the ancillary rights would limit it to the conditions at the time of its grant and therefore would not extend to improvement.

The court will only make an access order if it is satisfied that the works are "*reasonably necessary for the preservation of the whole or any part of the dominant land*"[3] and "*that they cannot be carried out, or would be substantially more difficult to carry out, without entry upon the servient land*"[4]

However, the court will not make an access order if by doing so it would cause the respondent's enjoyment of the land to be interrupted, or cause unnecessary hardship. If the court does grant an access order, it can also be subject to various conditions.

ANLA does not define specifically what type of works would be considered as "reasonably necessary", but as a starting point it does set out at section 4 a list of what are termed as "basic preservation works" which are:

> "*(a) the maintenance, repair or renewal of any part of a building or other structure comprised in, or situate on, the dominant land;*
>
> *(b) the clearance, repair or renewal of any drain, sewer, pipe or cable so comprised or situate;*
>
> *(c) the treatment, cutting back, felling, removal or replacement of any hedge, tree, shrub or other growing thing which is so comprised and which is, or is in danger of becoming, damaged, diseased, dangerous, insecurely rooted or dead;*
>
> *(d) the filling in, or clearance, of any ditch so comprised*"

The main issue with applying for an access order under ANLA is that, crucially, the order can only be granted for works which are

---

3 ANLA, s.1 (2) (a)

4 ANLA, s.1 (2) (b)

reasonably necessary for the preservation of the applicant's property. As such it is beyond the scope of ANLA to apply for an access order to cover any development works.

It is important to note that an access order can only be granted for works which are to be carried out to the applicant's property, not works which may be required to be carried out to the property owned by party over which access is being sought.

An access order can also be registered as a notice which will bind successors in title[5].

Breach of an access order

In the event that an access order is granted but the landowner will still not allow access then they can be sued for damages[6] with such claim being for any loss sustained as a result of the refusal.

3. Party Walls

If a party wishes to carry out works to a wall or structure which is on the boundary between their property and another separately owned property then they cannot simply carry out the work.

In such circumstances the party must follow the codified statutory procedure provided by the Party Wall Etc. Act 1996 ('the PWA') which not only governs the process of how and when such works can be carried out but also limits the scope of any potential claims which may be brought.

---

5   LRA 2002 Schedule 11 para 26 (2)

6   Access to Neighbouring Land Act 1992, s.6 (2)

What is a party wall? Section 20 of the PWA sets out three types of structures which can be party walls. Firstly, a party wall itself is defined as:

> *"(a) a wall which forms part of a building and stands on lands of different owners to a greater extent than the projection of any artificially formed support on which the wall rests; and*
>
> *(b) so much of a wall not being a wall referred to in paragraph (a) above as separates buildings belonging to different owners"*[7]

Secondly, there is also a 'party fence wall' which:

> *"means a wall (not being part of a building) which stands on lands of different owners and is used or constructed to be used for separating such adjoining lands, but does not include a wall constructed on the land of one owner the artificially formed support of which projects into the land of another owner"*[8]

Although, it is important to note that a party fence wall does not extend to a fence.

Finally, and thirdly, there is also a "party structure" which "*means a party wall and also a floor partition or other structure separating buildings or parts of buildings approached solely by separate staircases or separate entrances*"[9].

So, if a party is wishing to commence work then the first step is to ascertain whether the work will affect anything which could be classed as a party wall or structure. This should be a relatively

---

7 PWA 1996, s.20 (1)

8 PWA 1996, s.20 (1)

9 PWA 1996, s.20 (1)

straight forward task since the common factor to all of the different structures is that they must be on the boundary between the two properties. If the structure isn't then it isn't a party wall.

The next step is then to consider whether or not the proposed works are major enough to be covered by the PWA. The general rule here is simply whether there is a risk that the works are likely to cause damage or structural issues to the wall. If there is any doubt then it will be appropriate to either (a) obtain the professional opinion of a surveyor on the point and/or (b) err on the side of caution and invoke the procedure under the PWA.

On the basis that the answer to this is that the proposed works are of sufficient extent to pose a potential risk, the party wall procedure should be commenced. This is done by giving the other owner notice, the amount of which depends on the type of work being carried out. For new building or excavations (which are covered later) the requisite notice period is no less than one month[10]. However, for works involving existing walls covered by section 2 of the PWA it is two months[11].

For works carried out under section 2 of the PWA the notice, which is called a party structure notice, should include the following information:

"(a) the name and address of the building owner;

(b) the nature and particulars of the proposed work including, in cases where the building owner proposes to construct special foundations, plans, sections and details of construction of the special foundations together with reasonable particulars of the loads to be carried thereby; and

---

10 PWA 1996, s.1 (2) and s.6 (5)

11 PWA 1996, s.3 (2) (a)

(c) the date on which the proposed work will begin"[12]

Upon receipt of the notice the adjoining owner has a number of options. They can either:

- Provide their consent to the proposed works which must be communicated in writing 14 days after service of the notice[13];

- Refuse to provide consent to the proposed works; or

- Serve a counter notice under section 4 of the PWA within one month of the notice being served (which essentially requests that the party giving notice initially carries out further specified works to the party wall[14] as set out in section 4 (1) (a) and (b))

It is important to note that if the adjoining owner fails to respond, or fails to provide their consent within the 14 day period specified in section 5, then a dispute will have been deemed to have arisen which means that the dispute resolution process set out in section 10 should be invoked.

To commence the dispute resolution process the respective parties must agree to the appointment of a party wall surveyor, or if that isn't possible, appoint a surveyor each who will in turn agree between themselves on the surveyor to be appointed. The surveyor will make an "award" which will determine:

(a) "the right to execute any work;

---

12 PWA 1996, s.3 (1)

13 PWA 1996, s.5

14 See Bridgland v. Earlsmead Estates Ltd [2015] EWHC B8 (TCC)

(b) the time and manner of executing any work; and

(c) any other matter arising out of or incidental to the dispute including the costs of making the award"[15]

The surveyor also has a discretion under section 13 of the PWA to decide who pays the reasonable costs of the award.

The award will be binding on the parties but it is possible for this to be appealed by applying to the county court under CPR 52 within a period of fourteen days[16]. The county court may then

(a) "rescind the award or modify it in such manner as the court thinks fit; and

(b) make such order as to costs as the court thinks fit."[17]

Problems can arise if the party proposing to do the works fails to comply with the PWA, for example either by not giving the requisite notice before starting the works or by failing to appoint a surveyor in the event of a dispute.

In matters like this it is critical to act quickly as once the works have been completed, there will be no remedy for the adjoining owner to stop the works, aside from a potential claim for compensation for any damage caused as a result. However, if no damage has been caused then there will be no remedy at all.

If the party wall procedure should have been invoked but hasn't and the work is still being carried out then if the works are not stopped on request then it is possible to apply to court for an injunction to

---

15 PWA 1996, s.10 (12)

16 PWA 1996, s.10 (17)

17 PWA 1996, s.10 (17)

stop the work until the process set out in the PWA has been invoked and a party wall award given. Whilst an injunction will usually be granted in the adjoining owner's favour since the other party has failed to follow the statutory requirements of the PWA, prior to applying to court it is important to be completely sure that the works being carried out are to a party wall, as for internal works this may not be clear cut.

The case of *Fattahi v Charles Grosvenor Ltd*[18] is a contemporary reminder of the repercussions which can apply where there has been a failure to comply with the PWA. *Fattahi* concerned a claim for an injunction and damages by an adjoining owner for damage caused to her roof and gas flue by building works carried out by the defendant's contractor in building a second-floor extension. The defendant had not served any notice as required under section 3 of the PWA. The defendant sought to claim an indemnity from the contractor. The appeal, which had been brought on the basis that the damages award would have arisen in any event despite the admitted failure to follow the PWA, was dismissed.

In recognising that the cause of the dispute was a failure to provide notice under the PWA, and in essence, a lack of communication between the parties, Mr Justice Turner stated:

> "*I am satisfied that the essence of the Judge's finding was that if the Defendant had complied with the requirements of the 1996 Act then, on a balance of probabilities, the Claimant and the Defendant would have come to a reasonable mutual accommodation in advance of the commencement of the works and would have achieved a level of subsequent cooperation which would, in turn, have meant that it was unlikely that the Defendant would ever have faced a claim for damages from the Claimant*"[19]

---

18 [2019] EWHC 3497 (QB)

19 At [23]

One additional aspect arising from *Fattahi* worth noting is that the defendant had sought to claim an indemnity from their contractor but this claim failed because of the defendants failure to follow the PWA which breached a term of the contract between the defendant and the contractor that:

> "*All other consents reasonably required by this Company [the contractor] to undertake the contract works including Party wall consents ... shall be the responsibility of the customer [the defendant]. If the customer fails to obtain any such consents and the Company suffers loss as a result, including any loss of profit, the customer shall be liable to the Company for such losses.*"[20]

Any party who carries out work to a party wall owes an adjoining owner a non-delegable duty of care[21]. If a party instructs a contractor to carry out work which involves a party wall and loss is suffered by the adjoining owner as a result of their actions, then it may be possible for that party to seek an indemnity or contribution from the contractor to any claim brought by the adjoining owner, but this will depend on the terms of the contract they have entered into and whether notice was provided under the PWA.

---

20 [2019] EWHC 3497 (QB) at [7]

21 Alcock v Wraith [1991] 59 BLR 61

CHAPTER FOUR
RIGHTS OF LIGHT

1. Introduction

A right to light is a species of easement which entitles an adjoining landowner to receive light through various apertures of their property.

To some clients it may appear strange (and often akin to reactions when told about the 'general boundaries' rule) that the starting point in English law is that no property, or building, actually has an automatic right to light. The property must have either acquired the right by way of an express grant, or via one of the three methods of prescription for the property to be entitled to the benefit of it.

The implication of this is that unless such a right has been acquired (or there is some other restriction, for example, like a restrictive covenant), then a party is free to build on their land in such a way as to prevent any light being received by their neighbour[1].

A right to light can only exist where light is received through windows or some other aperture, and the amount of light which is entitled to be received is "*that which is required for the ordinary purposes of inhabitancy or business of the tenement according to the ordinary notions of mankind*"[2], i.e. enough to enjoy a residential property or to run a business. Therefore, it is necessary to consider first what the nature of property is subject to the light before then considering what would be enough for the ordinary purposes of it.

---

1 *Tapling v. Jones* (1865) 11 H.L.C. 290

2 *Colls v. Home and Colonial Stores Ltd* [1904] A.C. 179

If there is no right by express grant then as set out above, it is also possible to acquire such a right by prescription. As many readers will be familiar, there are three ways in which a person can acquire a right by prescription but the most common will be either by way of lost modern grant or pursuant to the Prescription Act 1832, the latter of which has a specific regime for rights to light.

Broadly, for a right to be able to be acquired by lost modern grant a party must be able to establish that a property has enjoyed the light, without force or permission, for a continuous period of 20 years or more. However, the Prescription Act 1832 ('PA 1832') requires the 20-year period (or longer) to be *"next before some suit or action"*[3], which means that the period must actually be followed by some form of legal action to 'secure' the right. Therefore, if there is cessation of the right prior to any application being made then that application would fail.

There is also a further trap in section 4 of PA 1832 which is that a claim for a right to light can be defeated if there is some form of interruption to the light (which in reality is likely to be some form of building work) which is acquiesced to or unchallenged by the innocent party for a period of 12 months (or more).

A much cheaper, and quicker, method to either prevent a neighbour acquiring a right to light, or to interrupt an existing right without having a physical obstruction, is for a landowner to apply for a light obstruction notice under the Rights of Light Act 1959, which creates a notional obstruction and is registered as a local land charge. Once it is registered the 'interrupted' party has 12 months by which to assert their right to light by issuing court proceedings, failing which the notice will have interrupted the right and the 20-year period for acquiring by prescription will start all over again.

---

3   Prescription Act 1832, s.4 (as amended by Rights of Light Act 1959)

The process is started by making an application to the Lands Chamber of the Upper Tribunal who will consider what the applicant needs to do to inform others about the proposed notice and whether this has been completed. If the tribunal is satisfied they will then issue a certificate which allows the notice to be registered and served.

2. Remedies

If a party has acquired such a right, then if that right is breached the innocent party is entitled to an injunction to abate the breach, or to an award of damages.

Historically, the courts took a strict approach on granting injunctive relief in such cases and until *Coventry and Lawrence*[4] was heard by the Supreme Court in 2014 the courts predominantly followed the guidance from the Court of Appeal case of *Shelfer v. City of London Electric Lighting Company*[5] which provided that unless there were "exceptional circumstances" (in which case damages would be awarded) an injunction was more or less automatically granted.

To modern day practitioners this may seem the wrong way round but that is no longer the position following *Coventry*. In deciding that case, the Supreme Court refined the position and whilst it was acknowledged that in such cases a claimant was entitled to injunctive relief, an award of damages did not require a condition of exceptional circumstances before such an award could be made.

4 *Coventry v. Lawrence* [2014] UKSC 13

5 [1895] 1 Ch. 287

Damages are awarded on the basis of what, hypothetically, would have been paid for release of that parties right to light, or if that is not possible then to compensate for that party's loss of amenity[6].

---

6 *Tamares (Vincent Square) Ltd v. Fairpoint Properties (Vincent Square) Ltd* [2007] EWHC 212 (Ch)

CHAPTER FIVE
NUISANCE

1. Introduction

Nuisance is an umbrella term to describe various types of torts but can be loosely defined as an act, or actions, whether voluntary or involuntary, which has the result of substantially interfering with the use or enjoyment of another's land. Nuisance is also split into public nuisance and private nuisance albeit it is the latter that will be the subject of this chapter. The distinction between the two is that the former would, broadly, cover situations where the interference concerned the general public and which would be a criminal offence, whereas private nuisance concerns civil wrongs which affect private individuals.

A private nuisance has been described as "*a violation of real property rights*"[1].

The key ingredient for a claim for nuisance is that it is necessary to establish actual loss (by way of damage) for a nuisance to be actionable. That is, of course, not the position with a claim for trespass where loss is not required.

Potential types of nuisance is not an exhaustive list, and includes damage caused by tree roots, pollution, noise and an incursion of Japanese Knotweed. The causes also do not need to be as a result of actions over a period of time (although they often are) and can also arise from a single event.

---

1 Sir Terence Etherton at 40 of Network Rail Infastructure Ltd v. Williams [2018] EWCA Civ 1514

Furthermore, not only must the damage caused by the nuisance be actual but must also have been reasonably foreseeable[2].

The starting point in any claim is to establish whether or not the claimant has a direct proprietary or possessory interest in the affected land. This is because following the decision in *Hunter v. Canary Wharf Ltd [1997] AC 655*, these are the only categories of parties able to make the claim. This may present an interesting position in cases where nuisance has been caused by a tenant but not a landlord, since it is well established that the only party liable in a claim for nuisance is the party actually causing the nuisance[3], so the landlord would theoretically be off the hook, so long as he/she didn't authorise the tenant's actions either expressly or impliedly[4].

Because nuisance claims are actionable in tort, any claimant will not only have to establish a proprietary or possessory right in the affected property but also causation in that the defendant was responsible for the substantial interference and damage.

Private nuisance claims will arise where one party's lawful actions on his own land subsequently effect another. In the context of neighbour disputes common examples may include encroachment onto another's land (by buildings, trees, roots, plants), damage by pollution, flooding or fire, or by creating conditions which prevent enjoyment of the other land, for example by creating excessive noise or producing foul odours.

In cases where the nuisance involves encroachment or damage, it is only necessary to establish that the encroachment and/or damage has in fact occurred. However, if the nuisance is a condition which prevents enjoyment of land then there will not be any encroachment or

---

2 *Cambridge Water Co. v. Eastern Counties Leather plc [1994] 1 All ER 53*

3 *Rich v. Basterfield (1847) 4 CB 783*

4 *Malzy v. Eichholz [1916] 2 KB 308*

obvious damage to refer to. In such cases the nuisance will be actionable if it amounts to conduct which would interfere with the comfort of living to the average man in those circumstances. There is no allowance for someone who is extra sensitive.

When considering the comfort and convenience of the average man, the court will take into account the character of the neighbourhood[5] and consider the nuisance in the context of local standards.

In some cases, a course of conduct may be pursued by one neighbour with the intention of causing annoyance to another. If that is the case then that conduct will amount to a nuisance even if it wouldn't in other circumstances[6]. However, it is important to consider that in order to succeed with such a claim it is of course necessary to establish that the conduct was of a malicious nature and that may be difficult.

Damage caused by animals which are covered by the definition of livestock is actionable under section 4 of the Animals Act 1971 but smells and noise from keeping animals may be actionable. The position differs if the animals have been brought to the land by the party or have just increased naturally. The test is whether the animals would amount to excessive or abnormal user.

2. The Rule in Rylands v. Fletcher

The case of Rylands and Fletcher concerned the liability for damage caused by the water in a reservoir which burst and flooded a neighbouring mine belonging to Mr Fletcher.

The rule in Rylands and Fletcher is as follows:

---

5   Coventry v. Lawrence [2014] UKSC 13

6   Christie v Davey [1893] 1 Ch. 316

"We think that the true rule of law is, that the person who for his own purposes brings on his lands and collects and keeps there anything likely to do mischief if it escapes must keep it at his peril, and, if he does not do so, is prima facie answerable for all the damage which is the natural consequence of its escape"[7].

It was also restricted by the House of Lords to apply only in circumstances involving "non-natural" uses of the land by the party causing the damage. Further modification was made to the rule following the decision in *Cambridge Water Co Ltd v. Eastern Counties Leather plc*[8] where the House of Lords limited its application even further by imposing a requirement that foreseeability of harm would need to be established.

There are, however, various exceptions and defences to the rule.

Act of God

It is recognised that it will be an exception to the rule if it wasn't possible to plan for, or foresee, the event in question. However, because this can only apply in the context of a claim brought pursuant to the rule in Rylands and Fletcher (and not in the case of natural nuisances) its application is likely to be rare. It will, however, be interesting to see whether there will be further development of this exception in the future as a result of extreme weather caused by climate change and global warming becoming more common and widespread. The rule may also become effectively redundant since if more extreme weather events become commonplace, the class of events which must be on a scale significant enough to satisfy the test of being impossible to plan for will surely become smaller and smaller.

---

7   Rylands v Fletcher (1866) L.R. 1 Ex. 265 at 279

8   [1994] 2 A.C. 264

Act of the Claimant

In circumstances where the damage is in fact caused by the party who is complaining of the nuisance, then it will not be open for them to seek redress. However, if the damage in question was only partly caused by the complainant then it would still be possible for them to pursue a claim for damages albeit this is likely to be reduced by allegations of contributory negligence[9].

Consent of the Claimant

Whereas a claimant may have caused the damage himself, it may also arise that the claimant could have provided their consent for the object(s) which has caused the nuisance to be placed there. This will be an important factor to consider where the object has dual benefit.

Independent act of a third party

If the object causing the nuisance has caused damage due to the actions of another then the party who owns that object will not be liable for a claim in nuisance, unless those actions were reasonably foreseeable and no reasonable steps were taken to safeguard it from happening.

3. Natural Condition of the Land

The law around nuisance therefore provides redress for innocent parties in the event that a neighbour voluntarily creates nuisance effecting their land, or enjoyment of it, by their positive action(s) or by bringing something onto their land which is not contained properly and subsequently escapes. However, what if the land in

---

9 The Law Reform (Contributory Negligence) Act 1945

question could create a nuisance simply by virtue of its natural condition?

Historically, the position was that nuisance from the natural condition of the land was not actionable. However, in 1980, the Court of Appeal heard the case of *Leakey v. National Trust*[10], which concerned damage caused by a naturally occurring landslide from a steep hill adjacent to the claimants' properties, which was owned by the defendant. The claimants' claim, which sought injunctive relief, succeeded at first instance and although the defendant appealed, that ultimately failed. The decision in *Leakey* means that there is now a duty of care on a landowner/occupier to take reasonable steps to abate a natural nuisance which could originate from his land, with this duty being measured against what is fair and reasonable in the circumstances[11].

4. Japanese Knotweed

A particular type of nuisance claims are those made due to the effect of Japanese knotweed, which is a species of non-native invasive weed which is very difficult to eradicate and can cause extensive damage to buildings, drains, drives and walls if not treated properly. In particular, as well as being able to grow through tarmac it can grow up to 20cm per day and reach over 3 metres in height. The root network in itself can be up to 7 metres wide. In order for it to be removed completely a treatment plan is required which can last for several years.

Japanese knotweed is classed under the Environmental Protection Act 1990 as 'controlled waste' which means that it can only be dis-

---

10 [1980] Q.B. 485 CA

11 See Vernon Knight Associates v Cornwall Council [2013] EWCA Civ 950 (30 July 2013) for a summary of the authorities in this area.

posed of by registered, specialist, contractors at specific, licensed disposal sites.

Due to the significant potential impact the plant can have, since 2013 it has been mandatory to declare when selling a property whether or not it is affected by Japanese knotweed[12] and in the event that the seller fails to disclose that then they may be sued by the subsequent buyer for fraudulent misrepresentation.

There has also been an amendment to the Anti-social Behaviour, Crime and Policing Act 2014 which means that local authorities and the police can now issue a community protection notice pursuant to section 43 of that act which imposes requirements on individuals, which in this context could include a requirement to take steps necessary to control the plant, to take steps to remove it and/or to take steps to prevent it happening again in the future.

If an individual breaches a community protection notice without just cause, then they will be committing a criminal offence. This will be either subject to a fixed penalty notice (of £100) or if prosecuted, a level 4 fine (£2,500).

In addition to reporting the incursion to the local authorities to enforce, it is also open for any individual(s) affected by Japanese Knotweed to privately sue the party responsible for the incursion in nuisance and seek an injunction requiring the removal of the invading plant including its root system, even if there isn't any physical damage.

The leading case is *Network Rail Infrastructure Ltd v. Williams*[13]. The respondents, Mr Williams and Mr Waistell, were two homeowners with land which was adjacent to land owned by Network Rail.

---

12 Section 7.8 of Form TA6 Law Society Property Information Form (3rd Edition)

13 [2018] EWCA Civ 1514

Rhizomes from Japanese Knotweed on Network Rail's land (which had been growing there for 50 years) encroached onto Mr Williams' and Mr Waistell's land and they issued separate proceedings against Network Rail in February and March 2015 respectively seeking injunctions and damages for loss suffered due to the encroachment.

It was decided on appeal that Mr Williams and Mr Waistell could obtain a final mandatory injunction in their favour requiring the removal of Japanese knotweed but not an award of damages for diminution of value, even though this was in circumstances where the amenity value of the land had been diminished by the presence of Japanese Knotweed even though there had not yet been any physical damage[14].

5. High Hedges

High hedges can often be the cause of a dispute between neighbours, since a high hedge can result in light to a property being blocked out. Absent an agreement between the parties to resolve the dispute the affected party can seek remedy via private nuisance and by local authority intervention under the Anti-Social Behaviour Act 2003 ('ASBA').

Unlike the position with overhanging branches or roots there is no common law right to reduce the height of a hedge.

Part 8 of ASBA gives local authorities powers to deal with high hedges which affect reasonable enjoyment of property.

A complaint under Part 8 can only be made by an owner or occupier of domestic property whose reasonable enjoyment is adversely

---

14 There is a distinction between Japanese Knotweed roots and tree/hedge roots

affected by a high hedge[15]. The complainant will also have to pay a fee.

When considering what will amount to adversely affected, the LA will consider what is reasonable in the circumstances including the amenity value of the hedge and to the wider neighbourhood.

So what is a high hedge? Section 66 (1) of ABSA states:

(1) In this Part "high hedge" means so much of a barrier to light or access as—

> *(a) is formed wholly or predominantly by a line of two or more evergreens; and*

> *(b) rises to a height of more than two metres above ground level.*

(2) For the purposes of subsection (1) a line of evergreens is not to be regarded as forming a barrier to light or access if the existence of gaps significantly affects its overall effect as such a barrier at heights of more than two metres above ground level.

(3) In this section "evergreen" means an evergreen tree or shrub or a semi-evergreen tree or shrub

Therefore, for a hedge to be a 'high hedge' there must be a line of two or more evergreens (i.e. not deciduous) which are above 2 metres in height and which doesn't have gaps above 2 metres which affect the ability to block light. The statute does not, however, extend to the roots.

---

15 ABSA, s.65 (1) (a)

The first step in such situation is to ascertain who is the owner of the hedge in question. This may or may not be straightforward, especially as hedges are often used to mark boundaries and may straddle two different parcels of land. There could also be issues if the hedge had been planted next to a boundary fence or wall and has since grown around it making the original position unclear. This is often where historic photographs will be useful evidence.

Once the identity of the owner has been ascertained the affected party must take steps to speak with the owner to try and see if resolution can be achieved between them. It is extremely important that this step is taken since if such discussions do not result in resolution the next step is to make a complaint to the local authority under ABSA and they can refuse to deal with it if they do not consider that 'all reasonable steps' have been taken to resolve the dispute prior to the complaint being made[16].

They can also refuse to deal with a complaint in the event that they consider it to be frivolous and vexatious.

If the local authority does action the complaint then they will investigate the hedge and if it is found to be interfering they will issue a remedial notice under section 69 of ASBA to the owner of the hedge which will require the owner to carry out such acts as to reduce the height and prevent any future occurrence. The remedial notice is binding on the owner/occupier of the land to which owns the hedge and is registrable as a local land charge[17]. If the remedial notice is not actioned then that will amount to a criminal offence which is punishable by a fine of £1,000.00[18].

---

16 ABSA, s.68 (2) and s.68 (2) (a)

17 ABSA, s.69 (8) (a) and (b)

18 ABSA, s.75

It is important to note that there are limitations to a remedial notice as under section 69 (3) ABSA the local authority cannot order the hedge to be reduced below 2 metres in height, or its complete removal.

Alternative Remedies

In the event that the local authority does not choose to deal with the complaint and informal discussions do not resolve the dispute then there are a number of other ways in which an affected neighbour can seek redress for a high hedge (especially if the issues are confined to the roots as this is not covered by ASBA)

Self-help / abatement

The first is the remedy of self-help which may be of assistance if the hedge is overhanging or its roots are encroaching, into the affected party's land.

They can therefore rely on *Lemmon v. Webb*[19] and cut back the over-hanging branches or encroaching roots to the boundary. As ever, caution should be exercised when considering this option in this situation, especially if the location of the boundary is unclear or is the subject of an ongoing dispute.

Litigation

It is also possible for the affected party to issue court proceedings for an injunction and/or damages in nuisance as the high hedge would be interfering with and affecting quiet enjoyment.

---

19 [1894] UKHL 1

6. <u>Remedies</u>

Due to the nature of nuisance claims the primary aim of any claimant will be for that nuisance to stop and therefore the appropriate remedy will be an injunction. There may also be a claim for damages in respect of any loss suffered which will be on a tortious basis and subject to the usual rules on remoteness.

CHAPTER SIX
OTHER POTENTIAL
DISPUTES

1. Harassment

Under the Protection from Harassment Act 1997:

"(1) A person must not pursue a course of conduct—

(a) which amounts to harassment of another, and

(b) which he knows or ought to know amounts to harassment of the other."

In addition, section 2 states:

"For the purposes of this section, the person whose course of conduct is in question ought to know that it amounts to or involves harassment of another if a reasonable person in possession of the same information would think the course of conduct amounted to harassment of the other."[1]

Therefore, for harassment to be actionable, as there is a requirement for there to be a course of conduct there must be at least two or more events which amount to harassment and which the harasser knew, or ought to know, that would amount to harassment of another.

The Protection from Harassment Act 1997 introduced harassment not only as a civil liability but also as a criminal offence[2], with the latter being a summary offence punishable upon conviction by either

---

1 Protection from Harassment Act 1997, s.1 (2)

2 Protection from Harassment Act 1997, s.2

a fine of £5,000.00, a six-month prison sentence[3], or both. The act also covers the offence of stalking[4] which carries a higher sentence of 51 weeks imprisonment, a fine of £5,000.00, or both[5].

The civil remedy for harassment is an award of damages for "*any anxiety caused by the harassment and any financial loss resulting from the harassment*"[6] and/or an injunction to restrain the harassing behaviour. If the terms of the injunction are breached then the applicant will be able to apply for a warrant for the arrest of the harasser[7].

The breach, if without reasonable excuse, is serious as it is not treated as contempt of court[8] but a criminal offence which carries a sentence of:

> "*(a) on conviction on indictment, to imprisonment for a term not exceeding five years, or a fine, or both, or*
>
> *(b) on summary conviction, to imprisonment for a term not exceeding six months, or a fine not exceeding the statutory maximum, or both*"[9]

---

3 Protection from Harassment Act 1997, s.2 (2)

4 The act was amended to include the offence on 25th November 2012 by the Protection of Freedoms Act 2012

5 Protection from Harassment Act 1997, s.2A (4)

6 Protection from Harassment Act 1997, s.3 (2)

7 Protection from Harassment Act 1997, s.3 (3)

8 Protection from Harassment Act 1997, s.3 (7)

9 Protection from Harassment Act 1997, s.3 (9)

2. Anti-Social Behaviour

Anti-social behaviour is closely linked to harassment but encompasses more than just a course of conduct which amounts to harassment. Such behaviour is defined by the Anti-social Behaviour, Crime and Policing Act 2014 ('**the ASBCPA**') as:

> *(a) conduct that has caused, or is likely to cause, harassment, alarm or distress to any person,*
>
> *(b) conduct capable of causing nuisance or annoyance to a person in relation to that person's occupation of residential premises, or*
>
> *(c) conduct capable of causing housing-related nuisance or annoyance to any person[10].*

The ASBCPA has introduced as the main remedy in such low-level situations the Anti-Social Behaviour Injunction, or 'ASBI', which replaces the previous regime of Anti-Social Behaviour Orders (more commonly known as ASBO's) introduced by the Crime and Disorder Act 1998. For more serious behaviour, the ASBCPA has introduced Criminal Behaviour Orders.

However, there are only certain applicants who are able to apply for ASBI's which does not include private individuals[11]. Therefore, generally, an ASBI will need to be applied for by either a Local Authority, a housing provider or the police.

For further detail on ASBI's readers are referred to 'A Practical Guide to Antisocial Behaviour Injunctions' by Iain Wightwick[12].

---

10 Anti-social Behaviour, Crime and Policing Act 2014, s.2 (1)

11 Anti-social Behaviour, Crime and Policing Act 2014, s.5 (1)

3. Fireworks

Excessive use of fireworks can result in loud levels of noise and may amount to an actionable private nuisance. However, there are also additional considerations in the case of fireworks or explosives.

A landowner who stores or manufactures explosives on their land will be subject to the strict liability imposed by *Rylands*. In addition, keeping explosives in a dangerous place is an offence under section 5 of the Explosives Act 1875. That act also made it a criminal offence to throw fireworks in a thoroughfare[13].

The importing, sale and control of fireworks is now governed by the Fireworks Act 2003. It is illegal for anyone under 18 to be in possession of fireworks in a public place. The Firework Regulations 2004 also impose a national curfew banning the use of fireworks between 11pm and 7am unless it is a "permitted fireworks night"[14] when usage until 1am is allowed and subject to a noise limit of 120 decibels.

4. Trespass

Trespass arises where there is an unjustified intrusion on another party's land or interference with his possession of it and would occur regardless of whether or not he was aware of it. Although there is not a requirement to establish that the act, or acts, complained of caused actual damage the act(s) must constitute a direct and immediate

---

12 Which is also available from Law Brief Publishing Limited and can be found at: http://www.lawbriefpublishing.com/product/antisocialbehaviourinjunctions/

13 Explosives Act 1875, s.(8)

14 For example, on New Year's Eve or Chinese New Year

injury to the land. Trespass has been held to occur by placing a ladder against a wall[15], or simply walking onto the land.

There are a number of potential defences to trespass, which include:

a. Justification

   The trespass may in some circumstances be justified, which includes any statutory right[16] and implied license (which would arise when lawfully abating a nuisance)

b. Express license

   Trespass would also not amount to trespass if the access is pursuant to an express license being granted, but would not be a defence if the access alleged to be trespass in fact goes beyond the terms of the license or it has expired.

c. Limitation

   There would also be a valid defence to a claim for trespass under the Limitation Act 1980 which states that:

   "no action shall be brought by the person entitled to the succeeding estate or interest after the expiration of twelve years from the date on which the right of action accrued to the person entitled to the preceding estate or interest or six years from the date on which the right of action accrued to the person entitled to the succeeding estate or interest, whichever period last expires"[17]

---

15 Westripp v Baldock [1939] 1 All E.R. 279

16 For example, see Access to Neighbouring Land Act 1992, s.3 (6)

17 Limitation Act 1980, s.15 (1)

d. Unintentional entry

There will be no liability for trespass if the entry was unintentional or if it was for whatever reason necessary save in circumstances where the reason for the trespass being necessary was as a result of the actions of the trespasser[18].

5. Airspace

A dispute may arise concerning infringement of the airspace above his property. The starting point in such a dispute is that the rights of a landowner are limited to a height necessary for the ordinary use and enjoyment of the land and any structures on it. They do not extend to the limits of the atmosphere[19]. Subject to this restriction, a landowner is able to stop any unauthorised encroachment into the airspace above his property, including any trespass by trees, cranes[20] and telephone wires[21].

6. Excessive Noise

Excessive noise from a noisy neighbour may be an actionable private nuisance if it amounts to conduct which would interfere with the comfort of living to the average man in those circumstances, taking into account the character of the local area.

The Local Authority is under a statutory duty to investigate complaints made to it relating to noise made between the hours of 11pm

18 Letang v Cooper [1965] 1 Q.B. 232

19 Bernstein of Leigh (Baron) v. Skyview & General Ltd [1978] Q.B. 479

20 Woollerton & Wilson Ltd v. Richard Costain Ltd [1970] 1 W.L.R. 411

21 Wandsworth District Board of Works v. United Telephone Co Ltd (1884) 13 Q.B.D. 904

and 7am under the Noise Act 1996[22] and if the noise is above the permitted level (34 dBA if the underlying noise is no more than 24 dBA or 10 dBA above the underlying noise if this is more than 24 dBA) may serve the offending party with a warning notice[23], which will set out a time (which cannot be earlier than 10 minutes after the time the notice was served) beyond which if the noise continues above a permitted level then a criminal offence will be committed. Should the notice be ignored then the Local Authority can either serve a fixed penalty notice of £100 or prosecute the person(s) responsible which, if convicted, will face a fine of £1,000.00.

However, as the repercussions of any intervention by a local authority are clearly not likely to be much of a deterrent to a serially noisy neighbour, in some circumstances the affected party is probably better off by commencing a claim against the culprit(s) in private nuisance seeking an injunction to stop the noise which will require sufficient evidence being adduced as to the level of noise complained of.

If the excessive noise comes from business premises or from vehicles and/or machinery in the street the noise is more likely to amount to a statutory nuisance which is dealt with by Local Authority investigation and (if the complaint is made out) the service of an abatement notice.

7. Criminal Acts

In circumstances where another's actions or conduct may amount to a criminal offence then if this is not dealt with by the police or the Crown Prosecution Service then it may be possible to bring a private prosecution against the individual, or individuals, concerned. This is,

---

22 Noise Act 1996, s.2

23 Noise Act 1996, s.3

however, a specialist area and further reference should be made to specialist texts.

CHAPTER SEVEN
RESTRICTIVE COVENANTS

1. Introduction

A restrictive covenant is a promise to refrain from doing something in connection with land so as to benefit another's. They are contrasted with positive covenants (which require a positive action, or a requirement to do something) as they are 'attached' to the land and can bind successors in title in equity[1], whereas positive covenants do not. A restrictive covenant therefore gives the party with the benefit of the covenant a legal right over that land, which can be enforced in circumstances where that the covenant is breached. The scope of restrictive covenants is wide but a common example includes a covenant for the burdened land not to erect any buildings or develop the site.

The starting point is to review the covenant and its wording to ascertain its terms and effect, as well as the original contracting parties.

Once it has been established that the covenant in question is a restrictive covenant then the next step is to ascertain who the parties are. Restrictive covenants are always directly enforceable against the original parties but whether it is enforceable against their successors in title depends on a number of factors, which will depend on when the covenant was created and whether the land is unregistered or registered.

If the covenant was created before 1st January 1926 then a search of title documentation should be made in order to obtain a copy.

---

1 Tulk v Moxhay (1848) 2 Ph. 774

Unregistered Land

For any covenant created on or after 1st January 1926 to be binding it should have been registered with the Land Charges Register as a Class D (ii) land charge at the time it was given and against the owner of the burdened land[2].

A search can be carried out at the Land Charges Department of HM Land Registry using Form K15 and payment of a fee of £1.00 per name[3]. If the covenant has not been registered then it will not be binding on successors in title.

Registered Land

After the Land Registration Act 2002 came into force on 13th October 2003, to be binding any covenant must have been registered in the charges register of the burdened land as an agreed or unilateral notice. Therefore, to ascertain whether or not it has been registered it will be necessary to obtain, and check, the title register(s) for the burdened land.

Other Factors

When considering if a restrictive covenant is enforceable against successors in title then it is also necessary to consider whether the covenant actually benefits or preserves the value of the land in question. In order to do so, a covenant must "touch and concern" the land, i.e. be close enough to benefit it or preserve its value.

In circumstances where there is no land benefitting from the covenant then the it will be unenforceable[4]. It is also important to check

---

2   Law of Property Act 1925, s.198 (1) (as amended)

3   Correct as of 2nd December 2019

4   Dano Ltd v Earl of Cadogan [2003] EWCA Civ 782

whether or not the burdened land was in common ownership with the benefitting land since the covenant was granted, since that will also mean the covenant is unenforceable, even if the land was subsequently transferred to separate owners.

2. Remedies

The remedy for a breach of restrictive covenant is either an injunction or an award of damages, but only the former is available if a claim is being made against a successor in title of the burdened land.

Historically, the amount of damages which would be awarded was calculated on the basis of what the parties may have reasonably negotiated and agreed between themselves for release of the covenant known as "negotiating damages"[5]. Recent case law, however, indicates that the modern approach to calculating damages should take the form of calculating any actual loss on a compensatory basis rather than considering what hypothetical sum would have been agreed[6].

3. Other options

In circumstances where there is a dispute concerning a restrictive covenant the affected party does not just have injunctive relief, or a damages claim, as their only remedy. Other ways of resolving the issue include:

---

5 Wrotham Park Estate Company Limited v Parkside Homes Limited [1974] 1 WLR 798

6 Morris-Garner and another (Appellants) v One Step (Support) Ltd (Respondent) [2018] UKSC 20

a. *Express release*

It may be possible for the party with the benefit of the restrictive covenant to agree to a formal release of the covenant which may be on the basis that a payment is made to secure such agreement. Any release should be formally recorded in a Deed of Release and any Land Registry entries relating to the covenant be removed.

b. *Indemnity insurance*

It is also possible to purchase indemnity insurance to provide cover in the event that a restrictive covenant is enforced. This is usually an option in circumstances where it is not possible to ascertain the party with the benefit of the restrictive covenant and can also be a condition of a lender if the property subject to the covenant is being purchased. It is important to be aware that if a party is wishing to explore this option then they must not contact the party with the benefit of the covenant prior to approaching an insurer (at the risk of 'tipping that party off') and cover is more likely to be refused if there is a highly likelihood that it will be enforced.

c. *Upper Tribunal (Lands Chamber)*

Another option is to make an application to the Upper Tribunal (Lands Chamber) for (a) discharge or (b) modification of a restrictive covenant under section 84 of the Law of Property Act 1925 (as amended). The application is made using Form T379 together with payment of the fee of £880.00.

For the application to succeed, the applicant must satisfy at least one of the grounds (against all benefiting parties) set out in section 84 which are:

> "*(a) that by reason of changes in the character of the property or the neighbourhood or other circumstances of the case which the Upper Tribunal may deem material, the restriction ought to be deemed obsolete, or*
>
> *(aa) that in a case falling within subsection (1A) below the continued existence thereof would impede some reasonable user of the land for public or private purposes or, as the case may be, would unless modified so impede such user; or*
>
> *(b) that the persons of full age and capacity for the time being or from time to time entitled to the benefit of the restriction, whether in respect of estates in fee simple or any lesser estates or interests in the property to which the benefit of the restriction is annexed, have agreed, either expressly or by implication, by their acts or omissions, to the same being discharged or modified; or*
>
> *(c) that the proposed discharge or modification will not injure the persons entitled to the benefit of the restriction*"[7]

These grounds can therefore be summarised as (a) the covenant is obsolete, (b) the covenant impedes some reasonable use of the land, (c) the benefitting party has agreed to it being discharged or modified and (d) the discharge or modification of the covenant will not cause any injury to the benefitting party.

---

7   Law of Property Act 1925, s.1 (a-c)

The Upper Tribunal can also order that in modifying or discharging a restrictive covenant compensation is payable to the party with the benefit of the restrictive covenant with such compensation being:

> "*(i) a sum to make up for any loss or disadvantage suffered by that person in consequence of the discharge or modification; or*
>
> *(ii) a sum to make up for any effect which the restriction had, at the time when it was imposed, in reducing the consideration then received for the land affected by it*"[8]

d. *Declaratory relief*

Finally, if the extent of the terms of the restrictive covenant are unclear then it would be possible for a party to make an application for a declaration also under section 84 of the Law of Property Act 1925, which provides:

> "*(2) The court shall have power on the application of any person interested—*
>
> *(a) To declare whether or not in any particular case any freehold land is or would in any given event be affected by a restriction imposed by any instrument; or*
>
> *(b) To declare what, upon the true construction of any instrument purporting to impose a restriction, is the nature and extent of the restriction thereby imposed and whether the same is or would in any given event be enforceable and if so by whom.*"[9]

---

8   Law of Property Act 1925, s.84 (1) (i) and (ii)

9   Law of Property Act 1925, s.84 (2)

CHAPTER EIGHT
ALTERNATIVE DISPUTE
RESOLUTION

1. Introduction

Alternative Dispute Resolution or 'ADR' is a term used to describe various methods of resolving disputes without recourse to litigation. ADR comprises a wide array of resolution methods ranging from negotiations between the parties or the parties' lawyers to processes involving third parties such as mediation and expert determination. As to the latter, the Boundary Disputes Protocol seeks to shift the approach in boundary disputes away from the present system of commencing what is in the end expensive, lengthy and complex litigation to a system of resolution by way of expert determination, following disclosure of evidence.

ADR as a whole has steadily grown in importance and popularity over the years since the Jackson Reforms in 2013 and is now a key part of any case strategy owing to the possibility of costs sanctions being imposed in the event that a party has unreasonably refused to engage in such a process. Lawyers also have a general duty to advise clients on mediation[1].

There is now a long line of reported cases relating to ADR and warnings given to litigants about the potential ramifications in the event that invitations to engage in ADR are declined. In particular, *Longstaff International Ltd v. Evans (Costs)*[2] in which both parties had suggested mediation at different stages of the dispute but which had

---

1   Halsey v. Milton Keynes General NHS Trust [2004] EWCA Civ 576

2   [2005] EWHC 4 (Ch)

been correspondingly refused by the other party. Neither party were awarded their costs.

In *Malmesbury & Ors v. Strutt & Parker*[3] the court held that unreasonable conduct during the mediation itself was tantamount to an unreasonable refusal to engage in mediation, leading to a reduction of 20% to the claimants' costs. However, this decision could only be reached as both parties had waived privilege over the mediation which will not apply in most cases and therefore is of limited effect.

As there is a tendency for neighbour disputes to quickly escalate, ADR provides a very useful tool to the parties to explore to see if the dispute can be resolved at an early stage.

2. Mediation

One of the most effective ways to resolve a dispute is by mediation. This is a simple process by which the parties meet and are encouraged to discuss the dispute and possible resolution by an independent mediator acting as an intermediary who is jointly appointed by the parties and is usually an experienced solicitor or barrister.

A mediation is a flexible process and can be structured in a number of ways. However, a typical format of a mediation is to start with a plenary session during which the parties sit in the same room and (either they and/or their lawyers) make submissions to the other side and the mediator about the case and their position. Following this the parties then return to their respective rooms and a series of private caucuses start with the mediator going to and from each parties' room to try and broker a settlement, or narrow the issues between the parties. In doing so, the mediator will often 'reality check' the respective parties' cases which can be helpful.

---

3 [2008] EWHC 424 (QB) (18 March 2008)

The decision as to whether or not to have a plenary session (which is optional) should be considered prior to the day of the mediation and will depend on the nature of the case and the parties involved. With neighbour disputes, which tend to be acrimonious and emotionally charged cases, having a plenary session could result in the parties becoming confrontational and aggressive which will start the mediation off on a bad note and may cause issues with starting settlement discussions. Therefore, it is often wise to avoid the plenary session and start with the private caucuses (with the potential to have a plenary session later on in the day, if necessary).

Mediation is not binding but is a popular and effective way of resolving disputes as the settlements which can be achieved can be more flexible than anything which the court can order. The process also has the advantage of being confidential as covered by without prejudice privilege and requires limited preparation - usually consisting of just a Position Statement and a mediation bundle containing the key documents.

Mediations can also take place at any stage in the proceedings, although in some cases it will be more effective to have a mediation post-issuance and within the framework of ongoing court proceedings with the ideal stage for the mediation to take place being post-disclosure but prior to the exchange of witness statements as there tends to be sufficient information for the parties to get a realistic idea on the strength of each other's cases and for meaningful negotiations to take place.

Another advantage to mediation is that it is relatively low cost. The parties typically pay for their own lawyers and half of the mediator's fees, which tend to range from £500 to £2,000 plus VAT.

A type of mediation which is particularly suitable for neighbour disputes is called 'community mediation'. This is where a member of the local community acts as the mediator and is sometimes offered as a free service.

3. Med-Arb

Med-Arb is a hybrid of mediation and arbitration and is where a mediation is takes place first but if any outstanding issues cannot be resolved by agreement the parties can agree that the mediator will instead decide on those issues in the capacity of an arbitrator and issue an award binding on the parties.

4. ENE

Early Neutral Evaluation or 'ENE' is a process where the parties jointly instruct a neutral third party (who is often a barrister or retired judge) to consider the case in detail and provide a written opinion, which may or may not be binding depending on what the terms of the instruction are, as to the likely outcome, with a view that the opinion will 'reality check' the parties and start settlement negotiations.

5. Expert Determination

Expert determination is a process whereby the parties jointly instruct an expert to determine, on a binding basis, a non-legal issue which is in dispute and is more suited to situations where there is no dispute between the parties as to the facts or the applicable law. This can be suitable for some types of neighbour disputes, in particular boundary disputes.

APPENDIX A
THE BOUNDARY DISPUTES
PROTOCOL AND
GUIDANCE NOTES

Protocol for Disputes between Neighbours about the Location of their Boundary (The Boundary Disputes Protocol)

1. Preliminary

1.1 This Protocol applies where neighbours are in dispute about the location of the boundary between their properties. It applies both to residential and commercial properties. It assumes that attempts to resolve the dispute by informal discussions have failed, and that a more structured dispute resolution process is therefore needed.

1.2 The aim of this Protocol is to provide such a process, which seeks to ensure that neighbours exchange sufficient information in a timely manner to minimise the scope for disputes between them; and to enable any such disputes to be readily resolved, keeping costs to a minimum.

1.3 Boundary disputes usually involve issues both of legal interpretation and of surveying judgement. Adjoining owners should bear in mind that, in order to investigate these matters properly, legal and surveying advice may well be required, and that the cost of obtaining such advice is frequently out of all proportion to the value of the land at issue.

1.4 It is not the function of this Protocol to provide advice to the parties. However, some guidance is set out in the accompanying Guidance Note and the Supplementary Guidance Note. Land Registry Practice Guides also provide useful guidance – see Useful Links.

1.5 If there is a dispute about the location of the boundary, or there is reason to believe that there might be one, neither party should interfere with any physical feature which might be a boundary feature, or with any land (or anything on the land) which the other party claims to be theirs, until after the dispute has been resolved. Both parties (and any professional advisers) should avoid doing anything else which might unnecessarily exacerbate the relationship between the parties, and/or which might increase costs unnecessarily.

2. Exchange of Information

2.1 As soon as it appears that there is a dispute about the location of the boundary, the parties can agree to adopt this Boundary Disputes Protocol. The date on which this occurs will be referred to hereafter as the Start Date.

2.2 Dates by which certain steps are to be taken are set out below, by reference to the Start Date. If at any stage either party cannot comply with the timetable, they should notify the other as soon as possible of the reason for that, and, if there is a good reason, the parties should seek to agree a revised timetable.

2.3 Within 2 weeks of the Start Date, the parties should:

(a) if their property is registered, provide the other party with official copies of the Land Registry title information relating to their own property; and

(b) seek to agree whether any determined boundary exists, or whether there is any note about a boundary agreement in the official copies. If there is, then no further steps should need to be taken, because such information should resolve the dispute[1].

2.4 If the dispute is not resolved at that stage, each party should assemble all the information they have in their possession, or which they can procure, within 4 weeks of the Start Date. This will include:

(a) past conveyances of either property (for example in a deed packet given to them on purchase, or held by their solicitor or lender);

(b) any further conveyances which are referred to in the official copies relating to their property which they are able to obtain, for example from the Land Registry;

(c) Photographs of either property which show the disputed boundary features.

The parties should exchange copies of such documents within 4 weeks of the Start Date[2].

2.5 At the same time, if either party considers that they may have an adverse possession claim which will render further investigation of the paper title position pointless, they must inform the other party, and set out the basis for their claim, supplying the following information:

(a) a description or plan of the area which that party claims is or has been in in their possession;

(b) the period during which it is claimed that the land has been in the possession of the party or their predecessor, and whether the claim is an "old-style" claim or a "new-style" claim. (This is explained in the <u>Guidance Note</u>.)

(c) if the claim is a "new-style" claim, the basis for contending that the party had a reasonable belief that the land belonged to them, or, if they do not rely on the third condition in Schedule 6 paragraph 5 of the Land Registration Act 2002, which condition they rely on, and on what basis.

2.6 Where a claim for adverse possession is made (whether a "new style" claim or an "old style" claim: see the Guidance Note), or where one party relies on a historic boundary agreement, the other party should explain the basis for opposing this claim within 6 weeks of the Start Date.

2.7 Within 7 weeks of the Start Date, the parties should:

(a) seek to agree whether they have the first conveyance by which the properties passed into separate ownership ("the First Conveyance"), and if so, which one it is; and

(b) if they do not have the First Conveyance, discuss what other steps can or should be taken, when and by whom, in order to find the First Conveyance;

(c) seek to agree, if an adverse possession/boundary agreement claim is made, whether to proceed to investigate the paper title position, the adverse possession claim/boundary agreement, or both.

3. Appointment of professional advisers / Negotiation

3.1 Many boundary disputes will involve a claim for adverse possession. This is a complex and specialist area. Anyone claiming adverse possession should seek legal advice as soon as they appreciate that an adverse possession claim is likely to arise to make sure that their position is protected: see the Guidance Note.

3.2 In simpler cases which do not involve adverse possession, the parties should consider:

(a) whether they can exchange information in accordance with this Protocol without needing professional input;

(b) having exchanged information, whether they can reach an acceptable resolution by direct negotiation or with the assistance of a mediator before incurring the cost of legal and surveying advice, bearing in mind the value of the land at stake, even if that means accepting something less than they would ideally like. In preparation for such a negotiation or mediation, the parties should ascertain (preferably by asking the advisers that they will retain if the dispute cannot be settled) what costs they will incur if the matter cannot be settled.

3.3 In all cases, the parties should within 8 weeks of the Start Date discuss whether they wish to negotiate or mediate at this stage, or proceed with the next steps in the Protocol.

3.4 If legal advisers are not instructed on both sides within 8 weeks of the Start Date, but are subsequently instructed, the legal advisers should consider whether a further negotiation or mediation is appropriate, and inform the other party, within 2 weeks of appointment. If agreement is not reached at that stage, the parties and the legal advisers should keep under review whether a further negotiation or mediation is appropriate.

4. The Paper Title Claim

4.1 Once the First Conveyance has been identified, each party must consider what evidence they will be able to adduce about the physical features which existed on the ground at the date when the First Conveyance occurred (and any other relevant issues of fact). The parties should exchange any documentary evidence they have (eg old photographs/aerial photographs), and identify the proposed witnesses of fact, and what they will say, within 3 weeks of the date when the First Conveyance is identified.

4.2 If the First Conveyance provides accurate plans, and the parties cannot settle the dispute, it is likely that expert surveying evidence will be needed. In some cases, other types of expert evidence will also be needed, for example, to assist in the interpretation of aerial photographs. For convenience, all such experts are hereafter referred to in this Protocol as "the expert".

4.3 In most cases where boundaries between gardens are disputed, and in some other cases, it will not be proportionate for the parties to have an expert each. In these cases, an expert should be jointly appointed (which means the expert owes the same duties to both parties, and the parties share the costs). The expert should be instructed within 5 weeks of the date when the First Conveyance is identified, and should be asked to produce a short report within a further 4 weeks. Instructions should be given on the basis of <u>Part 35.3 of the Civil Procedure Rules (CPR)</u>.

4.4 A jointly appointed expert who is a surveyor should carry out the following tasks:

  (a) produce an accurate, computerised, plan of the physical features existing on the ground at the date of inspection;

(b) plot onto that plan the line shown on the First Conveyance plan, or, if there is more than one possible interpretation, the various possible boundary lines;

(c) explain why the various possible boundary lines arise – ie what interpretation of the First Conveyance and/or the other evidence leads to that line being chosen; and

(d) produce any photographs which the expert considers will assist.

4.5 In other cases (for instance, where there are proposals to develop one or both of the properties and the precise location of the boundary is important for the development proposals), it may be appropriate for the parties to instruct an expert each. Instructions to the experts should be given within 5 weeks of the date when the First Conveyance is identified. As above, instructions should be given on the basis set out in CPR Part 35.3, so that the experts are aware that in the event of litigation the duty of the experts is to help the tribunal which decides the dispute on matters within their expertise and that this duty overrides any obligation to the person from whom instructions are received or by whom they are paid.

4.6 Short reports should be exchanged within 4 weeks after instructions are provided to single experts. The experts should, within 2 weeks of the exchange of reports, have a discussion in order to identify to what extent they are able to agree, and agree a short summary of their discussion which should be provided to both parties.

4.7 Whether an expert is a single joint expert or an expert instructed by one party, they should be provided with everything which the parties have exchanged in accordance with the Boundary Disputes Protocol.

4.8 Further guidance about what to expect from surveyors can be found in the <u>Supplementary Guidance Note</u>.

5. Adverse possession

5.1 Where this issue arises, each party should, within 14 weeks of the Start Date, provide to the other party all relevant documentary evidence and information about who the witnesses of fact will be and what they will say. Relevant documentary evidence might include photographs, aerial photographs, and receipts for works done on the boundary.

5.2 In some cases, expert evidence may be necessary - for example, if there is a difference of interpretation of plans, or there are aerial photographs. In cases where a boundary between gardens is disputed, it will usually be appropriate for the parties jointly to instruct a single expert. This may also be appropriate in other cases. In some cases, it may be proportionate for each party to instruct their own expert. In either case, the expert or experts should be appointed within 16 weeks of the Start Date, and should be asked to report within 4 weeks of their appointment. If each party has an expert, the experts should, within 2 weeks of the exchange of reports, have a discussion in order to identify to what extent they are able to agree, and agree a short summary of their discussion which should be transmitted to both parties.

6. Dispute Resolution

6.1 The parties should meet again within 2 weeks of the date on which the last of the steps set out above is taken, in order to see whether they are able to agree the boundary. If possible, that meeting should take place at the location of the disputed boundary with the expert (or experts if more than one was instructed). Any discussions should be on the basis that they are "without prejudice" and so cannot be relied upon in subsequent legal proceedings, unless a binding agreement is reached: see section 7 below.

6.2 If they cannot reach an agreement in principle, the parties should consider whether some form of alternative dispute resolution procedure would be more suitable than litigation and, if so, endeavour to agree which form to adopt. The options for resolving disputes without litigation include:

(a) arbitration by a suitably qualified and experienced lawyer or surveyor agreed upon by the parties or appointed in default of agreement from the Property Panel of the Chartered Institute of Arbitrators by the President of that Institute;

(b) expert determination by an independent third party (for example, a barrister, solicitor or surveyor experienced in the relevant field); or

(c) mediation – a form of facilitated negotiation assisted by an independent neutral party.

6.3 If the parties cannot reach agreement after complying with this Protocol then the final step will be for the dispute to be referred to the appropriate tribunal; either the Court or (by way of a Land Registry application) the First-tier Tribunal (Property Chamber) (Land Registration) for determination. Parties should be aware however of the substantial costs consequences of taking such action and that the risk of paying costs may be greater if they have failed to take steps equivalent to those set out in this Protocol, particularly alternative dispute resolution.

7. Agreement

7.1 In reaching an agreement, it is important that the parties are clear about what is being agreed. Agreements can be reached by reference to lines on plans or lines on the ground. If the parties are negotiating by reference to a line on a plan, they should be clear that they understand where on the ground this line will lie. It is generally wise to negotiate by reference to a line on the ground (ie to mark out on the ground the line being proposed), to ensure that there are no misunderstandings.

7.2 It is also important for the parties to be clear, if "an agreement" is reached on site or during the course of a without prejudice meeting, whether the agreement is intended to be immediately binding (and followed by a written document recording the agreement); or whether it is intended that the agreement will not be binding until a written document is executed. It is suggested that the former will often be more satisfactory.

7.3 If the parties reach an agreement (or an agreement in principle) by reference to a line "on the ground":

(a) The parties should ensure that the line is marked, by stakes where it does not accord with existing physical features, at the time they reach their agreement. As disputes are often about a few inches of land, the parties should make sure that they agree on which side of the stakes the boundary lies.

(b) The expert (or experts – or if none have previously been instructed, a jointly instructed expert) should be instructed to survey the line agreed, and produce a plan within 1 week, showing the agreed boundary line coloured in red.

7.4 Conversely, if the parties reach an agreement (or an agreement in principle) by reference to a plan, unless the line follows an existing physical feature, the expert (or experts if more than one was instructed) should be instructed to transpose the line on the plan onto the ground, for example, by placing stakes along it, in order to bring home to the parties, for the avoidance of doubt, the position of the line in relation to existing physical features.

7.5 In all cases a written document setting out what has been agreed will be required. The parties should annex the plan to a written agreement and record that in order to settle a dispute as to the location of the boundary, the parties have agreed that it should run along the line shown, for example, coloured red on the plan annexed. It will often be wise to have the agreement drawn up by a lawyer.

7.6 Each party should apply to Land Registry to note the agreement against their titles.

Written by:

Stephanie Tozer

Guy Fetherstonhaugh QC

Jonathan Karas QC

Nicholas Cheffings

Mathew Ditchburn

Date:

September 2017

Guidance Note

The following guidance is provided to assist people in dispute with their neighbours about the location of the boundary between their properties, and should be read with the Boundary Disputes Protocol. Although the authors of this Note and the accompanying Protocol consider that their contents provide a proper template for the resolution of boundary disputes, they are not giving legal advice, and do not accept responsibility for the contents.

Paper Title – The First Conveyance

1. Ownership of most properties is registered at the Land Registry. It can therefore be tempting, when a boundary dispute arises, to start by looking at the title plan produced by the Land Registry. That is not the correct approach. In the vast majority of cases, property is registered with "general boundaries" only. In these cases, the Land Registry title plan tells you nothing about the precise location of the boundary.

2. However, it is always worth checking the register itself if a boundary dispute arises. In a very few cases, a "determined boundary" (or some other detail about the boundary, eg a previous boundary agreement) is noted at the Land Registry, either against your title, or your neighbour's.

3. But, in most cases, the title and title plan will be of no help in resolving the boundary dispute. In order to find out where the boundary between the properties lies, it is necessary to go back to the

conveyance which separated ownership of your land and your neighbour's land for the first time. It is important to note that that might not be the oldest conveyance in the unregistered root of your own title. It might have been a conveyance of your neighbour's land and/or it might have been much longer ago. **The start point, and in many cases the end point, for determining the location of the boundary is the interpretation of this First Conveyance, in light of the words used and the physical features present on the ground at the time.** In some circumstances, subsequent conduct/conveyances can also be relevant.

Historic Boundary Agreements

4. Any deed subsequent to the First Conveyance containing an agreement by the owners at the time as to the location of the boundary will be likely to be determinative. (It will not however bind third parties such as a mortgagee whose mortgage predated the boundary agreement and who was not party to the agreement.)

5. So too will any subsequent oral discussion about the location of the boundary if this occurred in the context of a dispute about where the true boundary ran (as opposed to an agreed variation of the prior boundary line, which would only be binding if in writing and registered).

Adverse Possession

6. The paper title line might also have been superseded by adverse possession since the First Conveyance. Two different types of adverse possession must be considered.

7. An "old-style" adverse possession claim arises if, for a period of 12 years expiring prior to October 2003, land which falls outside a person's paper title is in their (and/or their predecessor's) adverse possession. Possession means an appropriate degree of control based on the nature of the land, and an intention to keep out all others, so far as the processes of the law allow, which is manifested to the world at large. A person is in adverse possession if they have no right or permission to be in possession, but ceases to be in adverse possession if they make a written and signed acknowledgment of the owner's title.

8. A "new-style" claim will be appropriate if there has been a period of 10 years' possession of land outside a person's paper title during a period commencing after October 1991. Possession has the same meaning as before. But, in relation to these "new style claims", an additional hurdle exists: the person claiming adverse possession must also show that until very shortly before a claim is made, they reasonably believed that the land in question belonged to them. They should therefore seek legal advice about lodging an application at the Land Registry as soon as they no longer have a reasonable belief that paper title to the disputed land belongs to them. They must also show that there has been no determined boundary and the land was registered more than a year before.

9. There are complications if either property was let (whether on a long or short lease) during the period of possession. In this scenario, legal advice should be sought.

Settlement

10. Agreements settling boundary disputes often fail to achieve a final resolution, either because the agreement is unclear, or because it fails to record all matters satisfactorily. If there is any doubt about this, the parties should seek professional help.

11. The parties should also consider whether anyone else, such as any mortgagees, should join into the agreement. Again legal advice should be sought about this where necessary.

Supplementary Guidance Note: What to expect from surveyors

1. The Surveyor's Approach

1.1 Surveyors who act as expert witnesses owe a primary duty to the Court or Tribunal before which they are to give evidence. Even when not retained as expert witnesses, surveyors must act in accordance with their professional code of conduct. It is important that those who instruct surveyors appreciate this and that surveyors are aware of these duties at all times. This is particularly so in the context of boundary disputes where emotions can run high (particularly where people's homes are involved). Those involved in boundary disputes must be aware that their surveyors will be expected to act with professional detachment. It is important too that surveyors for their part maintain that detachment.

1.2 That said in adopting a professional approach it can be important for surveyors to understand the position of their clients and the underlying issues between them and their neighbours (including how the dispute arose). It is important too that they seek to understand the position of the other parties and their surveyors. If they do this and adopt a good "bedside manner" they may play an important role in diffusing what can be an emotionally fraught dispute while retaining professional objectivity. If you instruct a surveyor, the fact that he or she seeks to speak to your neighbour's surveyor and to understand their position means that he is doing his job.

1.3 This note is designed to help those involved in boundary disputes understand the role of their surveyor and what you can expect them to do. It will also give surveyors an indication of what has been found in practice to be a sensible approach. Although the author of this Note considers that its contents provide a proper approach for the resolution of boundary disputes, he is not giving professional advice, and does not accept responsibility for its contents.

2. The steps to follow – A) When instructed as a Single Expert (i.e. by one party)

*(also see Section 4... Single **Joint** Expert)*

2.1 Initial reading of the supplied papers

2.1.1 Where boundaries are in dispute the first port of call is usually a solicitor and the solicitor will provide instructions to a surveyor. In some cases, those involved in a boundary dispute might start by going to a surveyor (who will advise retaining a solicitor to deal with the legal issues which arise).

2.1.2 Instructions to surveyors may vary in form, from a simple email/letter to a full bundle of documents and correspondence or, usually, something between the two.

2.1.3 The surveyor should always read through the documents provided and, if any useful documents are missing, obtain them himself (or request that they be provided if they are not easily obtainable). At this stage it is not necessary for the surveyor to form any hard and fast opinions but simply to be able to visit the property and commence the owner-interview with some questions in mind.

2.2 The initial interview with the owner

2.2.2 The first thing a surveyor should do is to meet the owner and visit the property in question. The surveyor will explain to an owner on arrival at a property the surveyor's programme for the day and an expectation of when the results will be delivered.

2.2.3 The surveyor should explain that, once the initial interview and the guided-tour of the property have been concluded, the surveyor will need to be left on his own to take precise measurements and photographs. Any interruptions may cause the surveyor to lose concentration or forget to take (or mis-record) a vital measurement.

2.2.4 The initial interview is unlikely to be the same as an interview with a lawyer where note-taking is essential, but may be more like a relaxed conversation.

2.2.5 The surveyor will explain that, once the measurements have been taken, it will not usually be possible to enter into another interview or give an opinion on where the boundary lies (though the surveyor will reassure the owner if the measurements are satisfactorily taken or something has arisen which requires further investigation). The reason for this is that the surveyor is duty bound to provide an independent judgment, and until the report is written it is preferable that the matter should not be discussed further with the client.

2.3 The guided-tour

2.3.1 Before measuring up, the surveyor will usually ask for a guided-tour of the perimeter of the property and may use the opportunity to raise questions about features on the ground ("do you know *how long that wooden post has been there?*" etc.)

2.3.2 It is important to be discreet when viewing the boundary: if neighbours are likely to be in close proximity it is sensible that they do not overhear conversations or that anything is said which might raise tensions.

2.3.3 At the conclusion of the guided-tour the surveyor will need to be left on his own for the measurement process.

2.4 The measurement

2.4.1 In most countries in the world, boundary demarcation and measurement is the preserve of the specialist land surveyor. In England and Wales this is not the case, for two reasons. Firstly, there are not many land surveyors in England and Wales and, secondly, many boundary disputes are in heavily built-up areas where building surveyors can easily measure-up the extent of a property by conventional means.

2.4.2 Where a land surveyor is involved, it is the usual practice to use a tripod-mounted electronic measuring device to make a map of the property that can be produced at any desired scale from a computerised model.

2.4.3 GPS (Global Positioning System) is now widely referred to as GNSS (Global National Satellite system). In recent years the accuracy, and ease of use, of the hardware and software involved has improved. GNSS equipment can now be used in the process of preparing plans for boundary demarcation. However, it must be used with care and by experienced surveyors. The reason for this is that the accuracy of a GNSS survey can be affected by overhanging trees and adjacent high walls/buildings. A combination of GNSS and electronic measurement devices (such as Total Stations) and/or laser offset measurers is the most common way of carrying out site surveys.

GNSS survey results can easily be merged with OS Digital Data but the limitations of OS accuracy should be borne in mind when making comparisons between the survey results and the OS mapping.

2.4.4 Where a building surveyor is involved, the measurement is more likely to be carried out using tape measures and hand-held laser-measuring instruments.

2.4.5 Whether a land or a building surveyor is involved, it is important that the resulting map is computerised, can be reproduced at any desired scale and thus can have dimensions extracted from it.

2.5 The photography

2.5.1 The purpose of taking on-site photographs is to provide a visual aid for a future dispute resolver or a Court.

2.5.2 Photographs may be useful to identify important features shown on plans and reports. This will remove any misunderstandings at a later stage of what the lines and features on a map represent. Repetitive and unnecessary photographs, however, will not assist.

2.6 Analysis

2.6.1 Once the surveyor has returned to his office and downloaded/transferred the site measurements into a computer system (usually, but not necessarily, in DXF format), the analysis can begin.

2.6.2 Whether the surveyor is instructed to produce a full report compliant with the requirements of the Civil Procedure Report or a short report for the client's use, in preparing the report the surveyor should consider :-

2.6.3 The Land Registry Documents: these (the Property Register and the Title Plan) are useful in seeing the trail of paper-title (conveyances and transfers etc.) that the LR has seen and recorded, and in seeing (on the LR Title Plan) the approximate outline of the property concerned. It should always be borne in mind that LR Title Plans do not show precise legal boundaries; they show features which may or may not be boundary features and which, in themselves, are subject to the 'general boundaries rule': Section 60 of the Land Registration Act 2002.

2.6.4 The deeds: It is the deeds (conveyances, indentures, agreements, transfers, etc.) that define the extent of a property and this is referred to as 'paper-title'. These may not be available from the Land Registry documentation and inquiries should be made of the client or solicitors if the Land Registry documents suggest they exist but they have not been provided.

2.6.5 The deeds may contain dimensions within the text of a deed and/or on the deed plan itself. The surveyor should analyse all these dimensions, irrespective of their legal status, and attempt to reconcile them with his measured survey plan. The legal status of dimensions (e.g. the question of which has priority, a written dimension in the text or one that has been added to a plan for identification only) is a matter of law and not of surveying expertise. Aerial photography: Aerial photography is available from a variety of sources, typically going back as far as 1945, and is useful in illustrating features that existed before the current dispute evolved. Land surveyors have specialist training in aerial photographic interpretation involving the use of stereographic instruments that enable three dimensional views to be obtained.

2.6.6 Terrestrial photography: It is often the case that owners have existing photographs (perhaps of family get-togethers in a back garden, or of a new car in the front drive) and these photographs can often help in identifying background features (hedges, fences, walls, etc.) and pinpointing an exact moment in time. The surveyor should always seek to ascertain who took the photograph and on what date it was taken (and explain this in the report). The person who took the photograph may, at a later date, have to provide a witness statement describing why the photograph was taken and when it was taken.

2.7 Conclusion:

2.7.1 Whether preparing a Short Report or a full CPR-compliant expert report, it is important that the surveyor can sum his conclusion up in short sharp terms. In other words, it is the 'news headlines' that initially matter to the instructing lawyer and/or owner.

2.7.2 Copying and pasting long sections of the surveyor's analysis into a conclusion should be avoided; the skill is in summarising the key parts of the analysis and then, if the lawyer/owner needs to delve further, the subject can be seen in greater depth within the analysis or notes (depending upon what type of report is being prepared).

3. Meeting of Experts

3.1 If a dispute continues towards some form of arbitration, adjudication or litigation, it is usually the case that the expert surveyors appointed by each neighbour are instructed to meet and draw up a list of what they agree upon, what they disagree upon and items that they almost agree upon subject to some reservations. The idea behind this is that the nub of any disagreement can then be arrived at quickly and therefore it can save the parties involved considerable sums of money in wastefully dealing with matters about which there is no disagreement.

3.2 It is frequently the case that one surveyor is based close to the properties in dispute and the other is several hundred miles away. Therefore, to meet on site is difficult (and expensive) to arrange. Surveyors, like most professionals, have congested diaries and so finding a mutually available date to meet-up at short notice can be very difficult.

3.3 The usual way to conduct such meetings is by email. The advantage of this being that the surveyors do not have to be available at the same time, and they do not have to travel a long way to meet up.

3.4 Both surveyors will have been to the site of the dispute, will have prepared a detailed map of the site and will have taken photographs, so they both have the necessary data at their fingertips without the need to be on-site.

3.5 The usual procedure is for one of the surveyors to draw up a "Scott Schedule" (being a tabular list of items that are pertinent to the dispute) and to name it V1 (Version one). The surveyor can make his comments on each item and then email V1 to the neighbour's surveyor. That surveyor can add his comments (and any new items) and return it as V2. In the end column of each item the surveyors can write *"Agreed"*, *"Disagreed"* or (perhaps) *"Agreed subject to xyz"*.

3.6 After several versions being emailed back and forth the surveyors will have exhausted the items and issues and can sign the Schedule off and issue it to their instructing solicitors.

3.7 On receipt of the Schedule, one or both of the respective instructing solicitors may wish to raise further questions of the experts arising out of the content of the Schedule. Those questions and their answers will form part of the surveyor's report.

4. The steps to follow – B) When instructed as a Single <u>Joint</u> Expert

4.1 It is increasingly common for an expert to be instructed jointly by the parties, usually through their solicitors.

4.2 There are advantages and disadvantages of the Single Joint Expert approach. The advantages include reduced overall cost (because the surveyors can make one large plan to cover both properties and carry out the analysis using all available documents) and the probability that the expert may not be required to give oral evidence in Court (thus further reducing costs). A disadvantage (from each party's aspect) is that the expert cannot have explanatory phone calls or day-to-day contact with one party's solicitor. This tends to make the expert feel more remote and detached from the process. However, from the expert surveyor's point of view, this may not be a bad thing in itself.

4.3 The most important difference between being a Single Expert and a Single <u>Joint</u> Expert is that the surveyor when acting in a joint capacity must be even more careful to conduct the matter in an absolutely impartial way.

4.4 It is important, therefore, prior to the site visit, for the jointly appointed surveyor to send the proposed programme for the day to each party. Typically, this may be as follows:-

09:45 Arrive on site and if possible hold brief introductory meeting with both parties

10:00 Visit Party A for discussion and guided-tour of the area of dispute

10:45 Visit Party B for discussion and guided-tour of the area of dispute

11:30 Commence measurement survey

c14:30 Complete measurement survey and commence photography

c14:45 Complete photography, dismantle surveying equipment, check notes

c15:00 Depart from site

4.5 It is also important to understand (and the surveyor should, in any event, explain this) that, with modern equipment, it is often the case that a survey map can be made with most of the electronic measurements being taken from one garden. In other words, there may be a location in Party B's garden from where 90% of the entire survey can be measured. If this is not explained, Party A may feel, wrongly, that Party B is being favoured.

4.6 Once the analysis has been completed and the report has been prepared, it is important that it is despatched so that both lawyers receive it at the same time/day. This can best be achieved by emailing it to both lawyers (i.e. addressed to them both on one email). However, if hard copies are required then, if both lawyers are on the DX system, then DX can be used. If one lawyer is on the DX system and the other isn't, then it is advisable to send both hard copies by Royal Mail 1st Class post to avoid a situation where one copy arrives the day before the other.

4.7 Written questions to the Joint expert may be prepared by one or both of the party's lawyers. On receipt of written questions, the expert should write back to the lawyer giving the cost of answering the questions and the timetable for answering them. As with all communication, it must be copied to the other Party's lawyer at the same time (i.e. the estimate and, once completed, the answers to the questions).

4.8 If the matter proceeds to Trial and (which will probably be a rare occurrence) the Joint expert is asked to attend, then the expert should sit separately to the parties in the Court waiting area and not communicate, other than with introductory pleasantries, with either party. If one party's counsel approaches to talk to the expert, then it must be made clear that both counsel must be present for such a conversation to occur. During the Hearing the expert will, in essence, be cross-examined by each party's counsel and then questioned by the Judge.

A Note on Surveyors' Fees

Surveyors acting as expert witnesses are not able to accept instructions on a contingency basis. A surveyor should provide a clear indication of the likely fees at the outset of each instruction.

5. A Short Report may be all that is required

5.1 A full CPR (Civil Procedure Rules) compliant report can be a substantial document.

5.2 The methodology that lies behind a full report it is that the surveyor visits the site, then carries out an analysis of the deeds, photographs, etc., and then draws a red line on the survey plan to indicate the probable boundary line. That analysis is usually complete before a single word has been typed to create the text of the report.

5.3 The surveyor will then spend considerable time typing-up the way in which the red line probability was reached and will attach and describe the supporting documentation.

5.4 The above process takes time and that generates cost.

5.5 It can be seen that the "probable red line" is arrived at quite early-on in this process and so it will invariably be more cost effective for the instructing (i.e. paying) party to be made aware of the result of the surveyor's analysis without generating all the extra cost of producing a fully CPR-compliant report.

5.6 With this in mind, a professional approach is to offer a "Short Report" option to clients. The Short report should include the plan (with the red line on it), the site photographs and a concise, numbered, set of methodology-notes (preferably on just one or two A4 sheets). The notes should also make it clear that they do not constitute a full CPR-compliant report but that they can be upgraded to a full report, if required, at a later stage and at further cost.

5.7 A Short Report should therefore suffice for most boundary disputes in that they enable the party and/or their lawyer to appreciate where the expert is going to say the boundary lies and this enables the lawyer to engage in correspondence, discussion and, hopefully, agreement with the other party, without generating the cost of a full CPR-compliant unless the matter proceeds to Trial.

Written by:

David J Powell FRICS

Date:

September 2017

Updated January 2020

MORE BOOKS BY
LAW BRIEF PUBLISHING

A selection of our other titles available now:-

'Ellis on Credit Hire – Sixth Edition' by Aidan Ellis & Tim Kevan
'A Practical Guide to Coercive Control for Legal Practitioners and Victims' by Rachel Horman
'A Practical Guide to Rights Over Airspace and Subsoil' by Daniel Gatty
'Tackling Disclosure in the Criminal Courts – A Practitioner's Guide' by Narita Bahra QC & Don Ramble
'A Practical Guide to the Law of Driverless Cars – Second Edition' by Alex Glassbrook, Emma Northey & Scarlett Milligan
'A Practical Guide to TOLATA Claims' by Greg Williams
'Artificial Intelligence – The Practical Legal Issues' by John Buyers
'A Practical Guide to the Law of Bullying and Harassment in the Workplace' by Philip Hyland
'How to Be a Freelance Solicitor: A Practical Guide to the SRA-Regulated Freelance Solicitor Model' by Paul Bennett
'A Practical Guide to Prison Injury Claims' by Malcolm Johnson
'A Practical Guide to the Small Claims Track' by Dominic Bright
'A Practical Guide to Advising Clients at the Police Station' by Colin Stephen McKeown-Beaumont
'A Practical Guide to Antisocial Behaviour Injunctions' by Iain Wightwick
'Practical Mediation: A Guide for Mediators, Advocates, Advisers, Lawyers, and Students in Civil, Commercial, Business, Property, Workplace, and Employment Cases' by Jonathan Dingle with John Sephton
'The Mini-Pupillage Workbook' by David Boyle
'Planning Obligations Demystified: A Practical Guide to Planning Obligations and Section 106 Agreements' by Bob Mc Geady & Meyric Lewis
'A Practical Guide to Crofting Law' by Brian Inkster

'A Practical Guide to the Landlord and Tenant Act 1954: Commercial Tenancies' by Richard Hayes & David Sawtell
'A Practical Guide to Dog Law for Owners and Others' by Andrea Pitt
'RTA Allegations of Fraud in a Post-Jackson Era: The Handbook – 2nd Edition' by Andrew Mckie
'RTA Personal Injury Claims: A Practical Guide Post-Jackson' by Andrew Mckie
'On Experts: CPR35 for Lawyers and Experts' by David Boyle
'An Introduction to Personal Injury Law' by David Boyle
'A Practical Guide to Claims Arising From Accidents Abroad and Travel Claims' by Andrew Mckie & Ian Skeate
'A Practical Guide to Chronic Pain Claims' by Pankaj Madan
'A Practical Guide to Claims Arising from Fatal Accidents' by James Patience
'A Practical Approach to Clinical Negligence Post-Jackson' by Geoffrey Simpson-Scott
'Employers' Liability Claims: A Practical Guide Post-Jackson' by Andrew Mckie
'A Practical Guide to Subtle Brain Injury Claims' by Pankaj Madan
'A Practical Guide to Costs in Personal Injury Cases' by Matthew Hoe
'The No Nonsense Solicitors' Practice: A Guide To Running Your Firm' by Bettina Brueggemann
'The Queen's Counsel Lawyer's Omnibus: 20 Years of Cartoons from The Times 1993-2013' by Alex Steuart Williams

These books and more are available to order online direct from the publisher at www.lawbriefpublishing.com, where you can also read free sample chapters. For any queries, contact us on 0844 587 2383 or mail@lawbriefpublishing.com.

Our books are also usually in stock at www.amazon.co.uk with free next day delivery for Prime members, and at good legal bookshops such as Wildy & Sons.

We are regularly launching new books in our series of practical day-to-day practitioners' guides. Visit our website and join our free newsletter to be kept informed and to receive special offers, free chapters, etc.

You can also follow us on Twitter at www.twitter.com/lawbriefpub.